STANLEY KUBRICK:
THE ODYSSEYS

Fabrice Jaumont

Books We Live by
New York, New York

Stanley Kubrick: The Odysseys © 2018 by Fabrice Jaumont

All rights reserved. No part of this publication may be reproduced, distributed or transmitted in any form or by any means, without prior written permission.

Books We Live by
360 West 118th Street
New York, New York 10026
www.booksweliveby.com

For information about special discounts for bulk purchases, contact Books We Live by

The views expressed in this book are those of the author and do not necessarily represent the views of the organizations with which the author may be affiliated.

Front Cover Illustration © Grafiker61. *Sunrise seen from space*. Illustration inspired by the opening scene of Stanley Kubrick's film *"2001: A Space Odyssey,"* from commons.wikimedia.org

ISBN: 978-1-62848-077-1 (Mobi)
ISBN: 978-1-62848-078-8 (Epub)
ISBN: 978-1-62848-079-5 (Paperback)

Library of Congress Control Number: No 2018954522

By the Same Author

Unequal Partners: American Foundations and Higher Education Development in Africa. New York, NY: Palgrave-MacMillan, 2016

The Bilingual Revolution: The Future of Education is in Two Languages. New York, NY: TBR Books, 2017 (also available in six other languages)

Partenaires inégaux. Fondations américaines et universités en Afrique. Paris : Éditions de la Maison des sciences de l'homme, collection "Le (bien) commun", 2018

Contents

ACKNOWLEDGEMENT 9

THE MINSTREL OF THE MODERN TIMES 11

THE RETURN OF ODYSSEUS 19

A CIRCULAR VOYAGE BEYOND THE STARS 35

THE ODYSSEY OF MOONWATCHER 57

ITHACA 87

STANLEY KUBRICK: FILMOGRAPHY 89

NOTES 91

BIBLIOGRAPHY 123

INDEX 133

ABOUT THE AUTHOR 153

Acknowledgement

April 2, 2018 was the 50th anniversary of a 1968 premiere screening in Washington, D.C. of Stanley Kubrick's *2001: A Space Odyssey*. The film remains the most fascinating cinematographic adventure that I was given to experience. I first saw it in France, in my early teens, and never forgot the impact it had on me, and the numerous questions it raised. The film certainly piqued my curiosity and made me write (and re-write) this essay, first released as an academic paper in 1995, and now, in print, as a tribute to the maestro, and in celebration of this anniversary.

My heartfelt thanks go to Frederic Colier and Books We Live By for publishing this text. Gratitude is also expressed to Professor Emeritus Daniel Becquemont at the School of Foreign Languages and Literatures, Université de Lille III for his encouragements and guidance at the early stage of this research project some 23 years ago. I have kept fond memories of my fellow researchers and professors, of my time at the Université and of the beginning of my own odyssey.

Fabrice Jaumont
September 14, 2018
New York

The Minstrel of the Modern Times

Among the numerous pre-Homeric Ulysses, the Ur-Odyssey is unquestionably Homer's *Odyssey*, a poem which engendered a proper literary genre: the epic–which has a particular structure, is lyrical in surface, and is profoundly philosophical. Homer's *Odyssey* mainly focuses on the Greek hero Odysseus (known as Ulysses in Roman myths), king of Ithaca, and his journey home after the fall of Troy. It takes Odysseus ten years to reach Ithaca after the ten-year Trojan War. In his absence, it is assumed Odysseus has died, and his wife Penelope and son Telemachus must deal with a group of unruly suitors, who compete for Penelope's hand in marriage.

The Odyssey has been copied, expanded, reworded and reshaped by numerous poets, playwrights, novelists, painters and other artists, who contributed to the mythopoeic inscription of the Homeric tale in Western traditions. Many authors were influenced by the Odyssean/Ulyssean narrative and owe a great debt to its creator. Among the most talented: Virgil, Dante, George Chapman, William Shakespeare, Pedro Calderón, Johann von Goethe, James Joyce, Nikos Kazantzakis, and Jean Giraudoux, to name but a few.

Each adaptation moves discrepantly away from the original version, and from each subsequent version, to eventually follow its own path and, sometimes, even produce contradictory or anti-Odyssean stories. Dante, for instance, substituted a personification of Odysseus as a centrifugal force in place of the centripetal, homeward-bound figure. James Joyce took complete artistic license with the original literary epic and, in the words of W.B. Stanford, "dislocated or telescoped the Odyssean order, and sometimes the analogies are rather far-fetched. But Joyce kept the parallelism in mind as a symbolical undertone." Nikos Kazantzakis adopted the non-Homeric hypothesis that Ulysses was an incurable wanderer who, after his return, set out from home to seek further adventures: a romantic conception of the Odyssean hero owing something to Lord Byron and Friedrich Nietzsche.[1]

The constant fluctuations of the theme of an "odyssey" may be explained by its definition: "a long, adventurous journey, marked by many changes of fortune; an extensive intellectual or spiritual wandering or quest"[2], thus inferring that changeability is essential within the Odyssean peregrination. The theme reveals throughout the centuries a parallel need for self-evolution and self-improvement within and without the narrative, in matter and form. To illustrate the conceptual versatility of the theme and the metamorphic propensities of Odysseus/Ulysses, W. B. Stanford writes:

> Turn by turn this man of many turns, as Homer calls him in the first line of the Odyssey, will appear as a sixth-century opportunist, a fifth-century sophist or demagogue, a fourth-century Stoic, in the middle-age he will become a bold baron or a learned clerk or a pre-Columbian explorer, in the seventeenth century a prince or a politician, in the eighteenth a philosophe or a Primal Man, in the nineteenth a Byronic wanderer or a disillusioned aesthete, in the twentieth a proto-Fascist or a humble citizen of a modern Megalopolis.[3]

A similar variability may be observed on the representations of the Odyssean theme in the visual arts. For instance, in the sixth century, grotesquely comic representations of Ulysses' adventures became popular on vases in Greece and Italy.

There are also many widely-scattered representations of Ulysses in sculpture, wall-paintings, engraved gems and coins.[4] Cinema has inherited from all these re-manipulations - whether verbally or visually - and has improved the theme thanks to its multi-dimensional possibilities. In 1954, Dino de Laurentiis adapted Homer's version in *Ulysses*.[5] In 1967, Joseph Strick attempted to transcribe Joyce's *Ulysses* into a cinematographic language.[6] In 1995, Théo Angelopoulos treated the theme in *Le regard d'Ulysse*. Stanley Kubrick's *2001: A Space Odyssey*[7] has reached a paradigmatic position about the Odyssean representation in the visual arts - equaling the works of Homer and Joyce by its originality - and is undeniably one of the best accomplishments in the history of film-making.

One aspect of the Odyssean theme, probably the most important, is the Return of Odysseus to Ithaca, his island, and to Penelope, this possibility having been denied by the resentful Gods of Olympia: the source of his motivations and hopes being found in his craving for home [8], his desire to round off his peregrinations, to loop the loop of his Odyssey. A circular, centripetal inclination is, therefore, noticeable in the layout of Odysseus's journey, even if - when observing Victor Bérard's tracing - sinuosity is more salient than circularity.[9] But, as we shall see with Kubrick's approach to the Odyssean theme, the "marriage of the sinuous line and the circle is aesthetically fortunate."[10]

Stanley Kubrick's Odyssey, as Michel Ciment labels it,[11] followed a sinuous path which began in New York in 1928. When young, Kubrick was very fond of chess, jazz and photography, three hobbies which, a posteriori, have been of relative importance in the treatment of his films: the fact that chessboards and chessboard-like floors are found in almost every film,[12] the musical soundness of each momentous scene, the exceptional pictorialism of a great number of shots might be sufficient justifications.

Kubrick devoured movies in theatres or in his projection room at his London residence. He avowed his adoration for Sergei Eisenstein, Charlie Chaplin, and Max Ophüls, and showed prodigious expertise on cinema and films. His gluttony for information and love of details; the years invested preparing for each film; his excessive control of production, direction, promotion; and his obsessive exigency with his actors, scriptwriters, and assistants helped him to reach a special place in the great hall of cinematographic fame.

Minstrel of the modern times, auteur, lyric poet and virulent polemist, this humanist possessed the powers of a visionary, and those of a strictly realist narrator. Original and independent, Kubrick (like D.W. Griffith, F.W. Murnau, or Orson Welles), is one of the directors who escaped Hollywood's demiurgic domination to accomplish his cinematographic Odyssey on his own. For Kubrick resisted the Odyssean ordeals of film making, and conquered the Golden Fleece of filmic independence: *Fear and Desire* (1953), *Killer's Kiss* (1955), *The Killing* (1956), *Paths of Glory* (1957), *Spartacus* (1960), *Lolita* (1962) made his freedom, the others: *Dr. Strangelove* (1964), *2001, A Space Odyssey* (1968), *A Clockwork Orange* (1971), *Barry Lyndon* (1975), *The Shining* (1980), *Full Metal Jacket* (1986), *Eyes Wide Shut* (1999) made his renown.

Considering the function and characterization of each protagonist, as well as each film's theme, plot, atmosphere, and denouement, Kubrick's movies follow a recurring logic, an Odyssean morphology, which film critic Jean-Paul Dupuy describes as such:

> Beyond their peculiarity, Kubrick's films seem to be connected by a strange similarity at the level of their formal treatment as well as the one of the stories involved. Each film depicts the Odyssey of a man who, from a world to another in an ascending movement towards knowledge, traverses the Power and the Glory to decline afterwards and end his fall on a recovery or death bed. Only at that moment a shot in slow or no motion emerges, suggesting a kind of backward return or circularity.[13]

Kubrick's exploitation and transcription of the Odyssean archetype and of its implied circularity into a cinematographic language allows him, simultaneously, to question the possibilities of cinematic spatiotemporality and movement. The circular stylization and narration revolving around mythical heroes–used at each level of his

17 *Stanley Kubrick: The Odysseys*

motion pictures–turns *Odysseanity* into Kubrick's singular technique, his signature. In his acclaimed book, *L'image-mouvement,* French philosopher Gilles Deleuze writes:

> Some large movements may be considered as being an author's own signature, which characterizes the whole film or even his entire work, but which also refers to the relative movement of such signed frame or such detail in the frame. A large movement, turned towards a changing whole, can also be decomposed in relative movements, in local forms turned towards the respective parts of a whole, the attributions to the persons and objects, the distribution between elements.[14]

As such, Kubrick's quest / questioning of spatiotemporality and movement equates his deconstructive analysis of forms, vision, meaning and language. The spectatorial receptivity and idiosyncrasies are central to the Odyssean experience or experimentation - *L'Odyssée de l'Oeil* (the eye's odyssey) as Kubrick-expert Sandro Bernardi calls it.[15]

On this visual experience, Stanley Kubrick and British science fiction writer Arthur C. Clarke, who both co-wrote *2001*, offered the following comment:

> When man journeys far enough into time and space, he will find things he has no right to see. But this is not the end of an Ahab-like quest on the part of men driven to seek the outer reaches of the

universe. Bowman is led into the time warp by the monolith that guides him toward transcendent experience.[16]

Each of Kubrick's feature films act like particles in a grand plan, miniature Odysseys united through a referential interlacement, forming an Odyssean craft which transports the spectator beyond his spectatorship, in an exploratory voyage through the arts.

The Return of Odysseus

On the several principles required to produce an Odyssey, the Return movement is among the most important: it completes the hero's journey, conforming henceforth to the traditional epic cycle. The Return also conforms to the cyclical interpretation the Greeks professed for Nature's mysteries, Time, Space or Divinities, and infers a subsequent circularity to the hero's destiny as well as to the Odyssey's morphology. Throughout the centuries of Odyssean composition, this conventional prerequisite of the Return had been adjoined a consequent sub-principle with regard to its artifactual configuration: most illustrations of the theme were to be reproduced on spherical ornaments, a structural juxtaposition and an aesthetic of the circle being therefore observed between contents and containers.

The same correlation may be drawn between Stanley Kubrick's movies and characters. The characters are points on the circumference of the movie, entrapped within their spherically circular motion pictures, but also submitted to the ellipsoidal logic of the Kubrickian invention: turning them into Odysseus-like weathercocks rotating around the axle of the scenario and the demiurgic eye of the director. The Return movement in Kubrick acquires a philosophical, strategic, aesthetic meaning, as film critic Pierre Giuliani writes:

> What is obsessional with Kubrick - the Return movement, the degradation movement - is not an artist's haunting thought but the strict obligation of the narration of the world.[17]

For, whether it is Davy Gordon, the declining boxer of *Killer's Kiss* pacing up and down, round and round, the station; Johnny Clay, the hoodlum of *The Killing*, obsessed with time's ticking; Colonel Dax of *Paths of Glory*, a pawn in his generals' self-promoted schemes; *Spartacus*, the rebellious slave and his fight for freedom; Humbert Humbert, the nympholept of *Lolita* and his secret affair with a teenage girl; *Dr. Strangelove*'s presidents and generals, inefficient in front of the nuclear conflict activated by Jack D. Ripper, the deranged general; Dave Bowman, the Odyssean astronaut of *2001*, and his mythical return; Alex, the juvenile delinquent of *Clockwork Orange*, brainwashed, manipulated and rendered to his normal state after his missed suicide; Barry, the Irish opportunist, reaching the high spheres of nobility to fall back to his former state of poverty in *Barry Lyndon*; Jack, the caretaker-writer of *The Shining* and his murderous frenzy; Joker, the Marine of *Full Metal Jacket*, and his journey through the military ordeals and Hell-like Vietnam or, finally; the sexually charged adventures of Dr. Bill Harford, played by Tom Cruise in *Eyes Wide Shut*. The Kubrickian characters have, in one way or another, to face the Odyssean circularity.

But, the same is true for the deuteragonists and antagonists, like Quilty, in *Lolita*, Antoninus in *Spartacus*, or Poole, in *2001*, or for the characters I call Telemachus, following their fathers' same circular path, as they themselves did after their own fathers–in Homer's The Odyssey, Telemachus follows Odysseus who followed Laertes, achieving somehow a filially perpetuated Odyssey.[18] Similarly, Brian imitates Barry Lyndon who imitated his father,[19] the duel proving a family legacy in *Barry Lyndon*. As Pierre Giuliani writes:

> Barry Lyndon, from Ireland to Prussia and Prussia to Ireland, the Return of a downgraded opportunist. Alex, in *Clockwork Orange*, following his own footsteps, repeating prosaically the stages of his progress. Following his own footsteps, this is very concretely - in backward motion - the exercise Danny Torrance is engaged in to escape his father's murderous insanity in *The Shining*. Jack himself, who followed the former caretaker's footsteps, the very one who murdered his wife and twin daughters. The Return once again, for Dave Bowman, the mythologically-changed astronaut of *2001*; for the liberal officer of *Paths of Glory*; for

> the rebelling slaves of *Spartacus* too, in a way, prompt to re-enact in an impossible, ultimate dispersal, their heterogeneity of the commencement.[20]

Spartacus's sole wish is to never return to slavery. In vain, for his last appearance on the cross, nailed to his fate, echoes his first appearance, chained on a rock, in the Greek-conquered province of Thrace, and vice-versa. However, his will for rebirth and *vita nuova* is indirectly accomplished in his son's birth and life, which has been granted freedom. Thus, Spartacus's Odyssey continues in his son's.

The little mechanical swimmer turning round and round again in a circular basin in *Killer's Kiss* remains the truest symbol of the Return movement, however infinitesimal it might appear in Kubrick's lifework. It fully corresponds to the mechanical Odysseus/Alex, who is tossed by the capricious winds of the Poseidon-like figures of authority that are the Minister of Defense, the *Droog*-like policemen and the subversive politicians,[21] to eventually end up his unbearable crawling by committing suicide:

> But Youth is only being in a way like it might be an animal. No, it is not just like being an animal so much as being like one of those *malenky* toys you *viddy* being sold in the streets, like little *chellovecks* made from tin and with a spring inside

> and then in a winding handle on the outside...
> Being young is like being like one of these *malenky*
> machines. [22]

After his suicidal descent he accomplishes an ironic rebirth into a post-Ludovico world, returning from the dead - from Hades - to begin his *vita nuova* re-incarnated in a narrator-traveler:

> I jumped, O my brothers, and I fell hard but I did not snuff it, oh no. If I had snuffed it, I would not be here to tell what I have told. I came back to life, after a long, black, black gap of what might have been a million years... As the music came to its climax, I could *viddy* myself very clear, running and running on like very light and mysterious feet, carving the whole face of the creeching world with my cut throat *britva*. I was cured all right.[23]

The image of the mechanical swimmer is appropriate to the Marines of *Full Metal Jacket*, whose turning round at the obstinately robotized pace of Drill Officer Hartman inside the dormitory equates their repeating - one after the other - the series of military exercises on Parris Island. The Marines are reflective of clockwork oranges, pressed by a de-humanizing system, of microscopic Odysseus training for a Troy-like Vietnam–their longing for home being sensed in their nostalgic rendering of the Mickey Club's song during the final scene.

The image of the mechanical swimmer is also applicable to Frank Poole, and his jogging in the large centrifuge of the spaceship Discovery; or the space hostess; or David Bowman, the epitome of automated man, who space-travels on his futuristic version of Odysseus's craft or off, floating in space and being carried away beyond the Infinite after his deadly combat against Hal 9000, the Cyclops, inside its computerized cave.[24] He eventually swallows a mouthful of hyperspace and drowns, to be revived forever in the eternally returning Star-Child.

The evolutionary ascension of Bowman - the representative of bow/Man - from his australopithecine to his robotized-dehumanized state and his absolute position within the Star-Child's celestial sphere coincide with his allegorical surpassing of the animal stage by means of his technology, from prehistoric bone to lunar shuttle, and his reaching the Superman - Übermensch - [25] by delivering himself from this very same technology. As Michel Ciment writes, "Bowman is the abstract man, in the Nietzschean sense, a bridge and not a goal, a rope drawn over an abyss between the animal and the superman."[26]

The connection between evolutionism and surpassing, Charles Darwin and Friedrich Nietzsche, is to be found in *Thus Spoke Zarathustra*, when Zarathustra addresses the villagers:

> I teach you the Superman. Man is something that is to be surpassed. What have you done to surpass man? All beings hitherto have created something beyond themselves: and you want to be the ebb of that great tide, and would rather go back to the beast than surpass man? What is the ape to man? A laughing-stock, a thing of shame. And just the same shall man be to the Superman: a laughing-stock, a thing of shame. You have made your way from the worm to man, and much within you is still worm. Once were you apes, and even yet man is more of an ape than any of the apes.[27]

This passage reflects an interesting association which Kubrick utilizes in *2001* to amplify the conceptual impact of the film, and, before all, to multiply interpretations and cover the tracks of his creation. The meaning of *2001* seems to be situated beyond both the evolutionist and the Nietzschean explanation.

The symmetry of the film does enhance the similitudes between the anthropoids of the Pleistocene era and the humanoids of the third millenary:

- The evolutionary ellipsis of the bone-spaceship achieves spatiotemporal fusion;
- The first touch of the monolith, similar for Moonwatcher and Dr. Heywood Floyd, magnifies the atavistic equation between both

chieftains;
- The gibberish exchanges during the fight between bellicose tribes around the pond echo the scientific jargon and the orbital banalities interchanged between Russians and Americans, around the circular table of the Hilton space station,
- The unappetizing food of the simians is equivalent to the baby's gruel of the astronautical homo sapiens.[28]

But, more to the point, the catalyst intervention of the monolith in man's evolutionary process reveals his unchanged incapacity to evolve without exterior assistance. Moonwatcher activates the *progressus in finitum* of Man by turning a bone into a tool after the revelatory apparition of the arbitrary, missing-link-like monolith and throwing it consequently "upwards", but by also using it as a weapon in his conflict over the pond, henceforth linking the progress of man to war, destruction and death. Consequently, the bone descends.

Similarly, the American scientists' intentions are destructive instead of instructive: by concealing the lunar monolith to the world, they conceal it to the Russians - a tactical revenge on the Russians' Doomsday weapon in *Dr. Strangelove* - to preserve their hegemonic position over their pond-like universe, a secretive policy which will cause the murder of Poole and of the hibernating astronauts. This also reveals two aspects related to the Odyssey of man: Firstly, man's chances for improvement are always given - a fact reminiscent of Homer, and the constant interference with the intervenient gods.[29] Secondly, the unaided man is unable to accomplish his Odyssey without galloping towards failure or death - as is the case with Barry Lyndon, or Bill Harford in *Eyes Wide Shut*.

Circularly beginning and ending *2001*, Richard Strauss's *Also Sprach Zarathustra* - known as the world-riddle theme and introduced by an ascending line of three notes: C-G-C - connects Nietzsche's threefold evolution to Kubrick's. Zarathustra, the wanderer-philosopher who incessantly returns to his cave, uses a threefold parable to explain the Superman. It is "the meaning of the earth to be found behind the thoughts and feelings, where the body is, as well as the self in the body - the Terra Incognita":

> To you I am stating the three metamorphoses of the spirit: how the spirit transforms into the camel, the camel into the lion and, then, the lion into the child... The child is innocence and forgetfulness, a new beginning, a game, a wheel turning on itself, a first movement, a sacred 'yes'.[30]

Another filiation is apparently to be found in the *Kubricko-Nietzchean* Star-Child, the Odyssey being a constant "new beginning", and "a wheel turning on itself" indefinitely. But, more to the point is the passing from the domesticated, manipulated camel to the rebellious, powerful lion in a moment of self-assertion and self-liberation, a theme recurring in most of Kubrick's films[31] and central to the Odyssey. In Homer, the Odysseys of Odysseus and Telemachus are symbolical of self-assertion and self-knowledge.

The journey beyond the stars[32] of David Bowman, the archer,[33] equates Zarathustra's Odyssey beyond his self, his walking stick being his spaceship; his intergalactic visions finding an interesting correlate in Zarathustra's commentary:

> Shuddering I would then fly like an arrow through the rapture exhilarated by the sun; far from the distant futures that no dream has ever seen, towards zeniths more burning than what any painter ever imagined, towards places where some dancing gods are ashamed of all clothes ... towards places where all becomingness seemed to me a dance of gods and a divine whim, where the world appeared unbridled and filled with liveliness and where it turned on itself; like an eternal flight in front of oneself and a new quest of oneself in many gods...; towards places where time itself seemed the happy mockery of instants. There did I pick up the word 'superman' near the

> edge of the path, and there did I learn that man was something to be surpassed.³⁴

Sharing similitudes with the Freudian theories, Nietzsche's abstraction corroborates the thesis that any Odyssey is, before all, a journey within the Self. As Gilles Deleuze writes:

> If Kubrick renews the theme of the initiatory journey, this is because any journey in the world is an exploration of the brain. ³⁵

Thus, concurring with Michel Ciment's assertion:

> Like any true odyssey, *2001* is a voyage in the exterior world which becomes a self-discovery. From objectivity the narrative moves to subjectivity, and when penetrating the memorial center of HAL 9000, Bowman embarks on a journey inside the maze of his own conscience. The spaceship "Discovery", therefore, leads him to the revelation of his destiny, and if Kubrick's film rejoins the Homeric myths as the title suggests, it is, like the Greek epic, the epitome of the interior exploration.³⁶

The 18th century room, in which Bowman terminates his "hallucinatory trip,"³⁷ resembles Zarathustra's place, the topos where "time itself seemed the mockery of moments" – for years are seconds in the room and growth is elliptic. The room could be allotted a plethora of interpretations:

- the room of Bowman's consciousness, a projection of his own personality,[38]
- a cage[39] or a cradle,
- man's last motel stop on the journey towards disembodiment and renascence.[40]
- An extraterrestrial observatory, according to Arthur C. Clarke.
- A laboratory where man's readiness is tested for a further, transcendental progression, where he is practiced a spectacular alchemy upon,[41]
- man's limits in his comprehension of infinity, man's nothingness and void.

Interpretations are endless. Is the room Heaven, one may ask? Is the Star-Child the Messiah of this millenarist, eschatological parable, the absolute sphere: *Deus est sphaera cujus centrum ubique, circumferentia nusquam*?[42] Or is it rather a *Deus ex machina*?

Agnosticism seems to be Kubrick's argumentative position against any religious interpretations:

> The God concept is at the heart of 2001 but not any traditional, anthropomorphic image of God. I don't believe in any of Earth's monotheistic

> religions, but I do believe that one can construct an intriguing scientific definition of God.[43]

But "God is dead"[44] and the parallelepiped monolith acts as a divine ersatz. The monolith is a *Tabula Rasa* pressed upon man's conceptions of spatiotemporal infinity and on his hegemonic position in the universe: man has no control over his destiny. A pessimistic undertone infiltrates Kubrick's scanty commentaries:

> If man merely sat back and thought about his impending termination, and his terrifying insignificance and aloneness in the cosmos, he would surely go mad, or succumb to a numbing sense of futility. Why, he might ask himself, should he bother to write a great symphony, or strive to make a living, or even love someone, when he is no more than a momentary microbe on a dust mote whirling through the unimaginable immensity of space.[45]

The room is also the end of Bowman's Odyssey, it is situated in an a-temporal nowhere, and Bow/man's first reaction - like ours - is to ask himself *Where am I?* A consequent anguish emanates from this *Where am I?*, echoing Kubrick's What am I? –an existential anguish already treated in *Fear and Desire*[46]. Oddly enough, Kubrick's words are very close to those of Blaise Pascal:

> When I look at the blindness and misery of man, when I look at the silent universe, and man

without light, abandoned to himself and like lost
in this corner of the universe, without knowing
who put him there, what his purpose is, what he
will become at his death, incapable of any
knowledge I fear like a man who would have been
carried asleep on a desert and dreadful island, and
who would wake up without knowing where he
is, and with no means to get out.[47]

Man's universe is insularly microscopic in Pascal and
claustrophobically anguishing[48] in Kubrick, in both cases:
Man suddenly realizes how infinitesimal he is in the
universe losing in one instant all reference points in the
immensity of space, to the point of losing himself and his
identity: Bowman becoming just man. "To know who I
am, I must know where I am," Georges Poulet writes:

> To know who I am I must leave from the place in
> which I am, and stretch myself indefinitely in
> spaces by my thinking, so that having possessed
> these spaces I could still determine with
> assurance, by the proportion that I have with the
> universe - when returning to myself, strengthened
> by my universal knowledge - where I am and what
> I am.[49]

But the 18th century room is a "nowhere" - a place to grow
in and die, within seconds, as life on earth. *2001* is a
pessimistic, intriguing, disturbing movie indeed and soon
becomes a circular odyssey of the thought in spatial
nothingness, a cosmogonist anguish, a mythopoeic

dereliction of the modern Odysseus.[50] As Michel Ciment writes:

> Anguish is at the center of Kubrick's lifework, it is also the propeller of his creative activity... The world of *2001* is on the verge of death and destruction, as is suggested by Khatchaturian's immensely melancholy music which accompanies the monotonous, empty existence of the astronauts.[51]

We seem to lose ourselves in *2001* and man loses his hegemony in the universe once again, or to use Alexandre Koyré's words:

> He lost the very world that formed the frame of his existence and the object of his knowledge, and had to transform and replace not only his fundamental conceptions but as far as the very structures of his thought [52]

The 18th century room appears to be Bowman's need for referential, geometrical points: an extremely square, symmetrical[53] frame dating from a bygone century in replacement of his computerized frame of existence. But what does the circular fetus mean, therefore? Does *2001* raise incalculable questions? A mythical explanation seems more likely to encompass a field of answers larger than an evolutionist or metaphysical one, similitudes emerging from these conceptual juxtapositions.

A Circular Voyage Beyond the Stars

There is a genuine analysis of myths and general consciousness in the Kubrickian representation. Like Joyce, Kubrick adopted integrative art, that is to say, a compiling of a wide variety of myths that are integrated into super-myths which encompass the others. *2001*, for instance, is profoundly Promethean: man's wish to elevate to the rank of God - in replacing men by HAL-like machines or in competing with the gods[54] - eventually leads him to his unplanned metamorphosis in a celestial, eternal sphere: an anodyne to man's anguish and his brief lifespan. The desire to be God would therefore result from a refusal of anguishing reality as well as a denial of mortality. As Philippe Sellier writes:

> The structure of the heroic myth implies a refusal of ordinary life, a wish for heroism, for superiority over the rest of the world, for a dazzling self-realization, for an elevation to a quasi-divine condition: the epic, which is the hero's progressive elevation until his eternal rebirth.[55]

Correspondingly to this definition, the Kubrickian hero follows a progressive elevation, in quest of an eternal rebirth: his solar elevation[56] conforming to the Sun's Dawn-Zenith-Twilight course. Bowman is undoubtedly a solar hero as his dawn-like[57] pre-historical stage is "enlightened" by an ellipsis over the monolith. Present at each stage of the hero's evolution, the Sun introduces *2001* and accompanies Dr. Floyd's travel and Bowman's episode. The Sun's rising is a birth; its setting is but an apparent death. Bowman, Alex and Barry[58] acquire this solar quality, their Odyssey following the mythical pattern: ascent-apogee-decline - or Christ's Ascension-Apotheosis-Resurrection, if one considers *2001* as a Christian or anti-Christian movie.

Besides, in accordance with the epic paradigm, this solar quality is marked by certain physical traits among which the eyes are prominent: the gaze discloses the hero's solar majesty - Heracles's eyes shot flames. An over-emphasis on his solar quality may also raise monstrous traits: his eyes would hence shoot flames.[59] The eyes are omnipresent in Kubrick, a voyeuristic relation occurs in most movies: Humbert's peeking at Lolita's body, HAL's observing every movement of the spaceship's inhabitants with his one-eyed omnipresence or the Star-Child's sphere-like eyes; Barry's piercing Lady Lyndon with a loving, poisoned arrow; Bill Harford's masked voyeurism during

37 *Stanley Kubrick: The Odysseys*

Eyes Wide Shut's orgies. But, more to the point, the monstrosity of the solar hero is certainly to be detected in the closed-up, glaring eyes of Alex, Jack, private Pyle, Bowman, all glancing at the screen - at us - in a moment of uncontrolled, alienated, fury.

Along the myth of the solar hero in quest of eternity is the myth of the Eternal Return[60], also developed by Nietzsche. The return of Odysseus[61] tends towards the Eternal Return, which is a questioning of time, and a refusal of death common to most heroic myths. The Eternal Return, as George Poulet writes, is a circle:

> One of which the only points inscribed on the circumference matter. Not the totality of cyclical time but simply the fact that, thanks to the movement of the cycle, each moment, which it is composed of, return an infinite number of times in the field of consciousness. Each moment of time is peripheral and central at the same time. Peripheral, since it is only a point situated at the circumference; central, since this point, returning numerous times to the same place, makes of this place a fixed and eternal point.[62]

The Kubrickian Odysseus is, in a certain way, captured within the movement of the Eternal Return, the character's fate being sealed off to a circular logic of time ticking and urgency, as in *The Killing*. The film builds on an involute structure of simultaneity and repetition, decomposing and recomposing its figures almost harmoniously, forming what Paul Valéry calls "an ornament of time" as the repetition of motifs, or their symmetry, would form an ornament of space."[63] The Eternal Return is also an involute structure of recollections, which links past and present through the medium of memory. It is observable in *Killer's Kiss* with Davy Gordon, the boxer-narrator, whose narration flashes back and forth between his past and present as narrator and the past and present of his characters, his memory's movements in time rotating like his round pacing in the train station.

The Eternal Return of the hero is also attained through a process of fixation, like the photogrammic permanence which immobilizes one point of Barry Lyndon's circular Odyssey, after he has stepped into a coach forever, or Jack's double fixation in time and space frozen in the maze and on the 1921 photograph.[64] Both examples project the heroes out of their story's temporality, out of their return - to Ireland or to 1921 - being halted, fixed, rendered unchangeable: the a-temporal return of Kubrick's Odysseus. By becoming a rotational sphere, Bowman achieves a-temporality, for a sphere has no beginning and no end. By turning on itself for ever, the Star-Child reproduces the constantly turning mechanical wheel of the space station as well as Nietzsche's wheel:

Stanley Kubrick: The Odysseys

> Everything passes, and everything returns, the wheel of the Being never stops. Everything dies, everything blossoms again, the year of the Being is eternal. Everything breaks, everything is repaired, the house of the Being is rebuilt eternally. Everything parts, everything rejoins, the ring of the Being remains true to itself everlastingly. The Being commences at each instant; for each Here the ball rolls to a There. The middle is everywhere. The way of eternity is curved.[65]

The Eternal Return engenders a paradoxical tug of war between centripetal and centrifugal forces, for Kubrick's Odysseus is enclosed within a superior spatial and temporal mechanism which activates his misunderstood rotation. Spartacus's conflict is symbolized by his chained revolution around and against the pole of slavery that he has always known, Humbert is chained to his life-long chimera, Alex is chained to his Ludovico conditioning which pushes him backward in time, Barry to his original roguery and to his place of birth, Jack is forever chained to the Overlook Hotel, Joker rotates in "a world of shit" without his knowing why, Bill Harford's jealousy or sexual revenge takes him through the darkest hours of his life. Any attempt at disrupting the mechanism seems doomed to failure, Kubrick's Odysseus having little control over his Odyssey. Fatality is linked to the Eternal Return of Odysseus, or as Otto Weininger writes:

To turn around in spite of oneself like Robinson is absurd; to live a new situation exactly the same way one has already lived is terrifying; to waltz round in the circle of a Viennese waltz expresses a fatalistic indifference; for an adult the brain game is harrowing; it is immoral to say twice the same thing, to repeat oneself... *No ens metaphysicum* wants the turning movement. What man - in so far as he is a man - wants is immortality in total freedom, but a state of being alive eternally which is a process of the world. Counter to this, the idea of the voyager and even of the pleasure of voyaging are founded on a genuine metaphysic theme which honors the time's unique sense of the man willing to be himself.[66]

Weininger recalls the Vienese waltz of Johan Straus's *The Blue Danube*[67] and the mechanical ballet of the Prater-like big wheel of *2001*, past and future reunited in the Eternal Return of the circle. This also evokes Alex and the Eternal Return that he accomplishes in re-living his situation in counter-clock order, till his renascent stage is reached after his missed suicide, which paradoxically disrupts the superior mechanism[68] which controls him. The Eternal Return for Jack and Danny who, by previewing their future situation by means of premonitory dreams or "shining" visions fuse their present with their future and their future with their past, both being proposed eternity in the Calypso's cave-like hotel.[69] Moreover, Jack's typing indefinitely "all work and no play made Jack a dull boy" conduces him to the limits of time which are also his own. As Pierre Giuliani writes:

> To the infinite of a right line without end, to the infinite of a vicious circle, to the infinite of a maze into which Jack disappears.[70]

Eternity might therefore be central to the Kubrickian meditation: the Kubrickian Odysseus reaches - in the ascending movement of Kubrick's imagination - a satellite position, orbiting around the director's omniscient, birth-giving camera.

Eternity is absolutely circular in Kubrick and the narrative circularity inherent to the Odyssean theme has become film rhetoric, a stylization which occurs at each level of the filmic creation. Conceptual and mythical circles are given a circular configuration, the Odyssean structural juxtaposition between contents and containers is respected, Kubrick's circular aestheticization encompassing every detail: from the image treatment to the setting, costumes and props. As Jean-Loup Bourget noticed:

> Clockwork Orange, proposes all the avatars of the circle: round hat on round head, moth or billiard

balls, the prisoners' round, the women's breasts, Mrs. Alexander's, in particular, which are peeled like an orange.[71]

In *2001*, the circle figure is the true representation of absoluteness and durability - as opposed to the instable, destructive, oedipal triangle of the Hamlet-like *Barry Lyndon* or *The Shining*. The *2001* circle is also the symbol of procreation and gestation - circles and corridors[72] converting the interior of Discovery into a well-lit-womb[73], which rejoins A.C. Clarke's favorite theme, namely, the qualitative mutation in human development and the notion of a kind of childhood's end for human history. As Michel Ciment writes:

> *2001* is rich in sexual images - uterine, ovular or phallic, from Orion, the arrow-shaped spaceship settling in the celestial wheel to Aries's sphere moon landing in a circular base. The Space Odyssey - the film of metamorphoses, fecundations and births - terminates with a self-reproduction.[74]

In *The Shining*, the Navajo circle[75] in which Danny's Big Wheels[76] rests is the very spot where Hallorann, the black cook, is murdered.

The circle is symbolic of the superior mechanism acting in, on, or under the hotel and controlling, confining, the residents to its circumference: the superimposition of circles - the Navajo's, the Overlook Hotel's, Jack's brain - transforming three-dimensionality into multi-dimensionality. The bi-dimensionality of the 1921 photograph, the three-dimensionality of the characters, the zero-dimensionality or fourth-dimensionality of the poltergeists' space haunt the film. Jack angrily throws a yellow tennis ball against a sand painting which, uncharacteristically, delineates a totally masculine world; within its enclosed design, which includes the traditional opening to the East, four males stand erect within the painting's circle. It is as if Jack were knocking on the door of time, which is the door of his consciousness if one accepts the idea that the hotel is the extension of Jack's mind.

This could also be the door to the underworld - Hades[77] - the Navajo circle being a protection against poltergeists.[78] As film critic Louis Hautecoeur writes:

> The circle is a defense against the spirits that might attack the magician. It is also a way of helping him preserve his strength in isolation, without exterior loss... circular liturgies destined to exorcise the demons and purify the faithful... circular pentacles... The circle appears on the ground surface and imposes a limit, a frontier to the underground divinities, but they are even stronger in their lairs, caves, and cracks.[79]

In *The Shining*, the voyagers cross the frontier[80] both ways until the fusion of both spaces (the spaces of the Over/look Hotel and of the Under/look hotel - which is a no-space) and both times (the times of Jack's family and of the ghosts - which is a no-time) becomes total when Grady, the unreal, opens the very real door of Jack's jail, thus announcing Jack's Eternal Return among his fellow creatures.

In *Eyes Wide Shut*, women wearing black capes and masks form a circle in a cathedral-like room, while a hierophant standing in the middle of the circle anoints them with a censer and taps the ground with his cane to make them bow, stand up, undress, and reveal their naked bodies to a crowd of masked individuals in a timeless, dream-like ritual. The circle opens the door of Bill Harford's underworld and make him quickly realize the problematic situation he has put himself in and cannot get out of.

The surface of the circular image is also correlative with the metaphysical iceberg-like undertones of the Odyssean process. In *Spartacus*, for instance, the circle figures are extensions of the characters' situation: the arena and the prisons are the slaves' universe as opposed to the verticality of the Roman columns, until the roles are reversed. Moreover, as a sign of separation between the two worlds, the bars of the gladiators' jail come to cover the whole screen. The double curvature of the agora-shaped senate room and its seats are at the center of the Roman spherical empire, the senators performing as Olympian masters of all destinies when associated with the chessboard-floor of the room.[81]

The circle is once again combined with a chessboard in the chateau of *Paths of Glory*. During the court martial, the three soldiers, who are tried for cowardice stand in a circle during the trial. Their judges are facing them. Separating the prosecution, Mireau and Roget, from the defense, Dax, the chessboard floor is the scene of a military game of chess: the stake being the accused whose life has shrunk to the circumference of the aforementioned circle.[82] As T. A. Nelson writes:

> Kubrick creates a cinematic chess game, reminiscent of both his earlier films and Nabokov's novel, which opposes Humbert's White to Quilty's Black. Chess, of course, superbly objectifies a state of paranoia and the themes of deception and entrapment; it demands from each player a constant vigilance lest he become the butt of an opponent's malicious joke. In Lolita, Kubrick allows his audience to watch the game from his vantage point by providing both privileged glimpses of Quilty's moves and, long before it dawns on Humbert, the knowledge that

> Lolita longs to be Quilty's Black Queen rather than Humbert's White.[83]

Circularity is associated with chess-like calculation as seen in the example if the Generals circle around settees in Mireau's lounge, followed by a camera movement which captures the circular, scheming logic of Mireau and Broulard, both spinning their webs around the Ant Hill's promotional possibilities. In *Lolita*, Kubrick creates a cinematic chess game central to the sexual battles opposing Charlotte Haze to Lolita, her daughter - Humbert being at stake; Humbert to Charlotte and to Clare Quilty, the lustful playwright - Lolita being at stake this time.[84]

A circular strategy is noticeable in Kubrick's movies - the circle is the scene of a fight between two opponents, circularity being automatically fatal to one of them. Examples include Davy's Boxing match in *Killer's Kiss*; Spartacus's combat against Draba, the Ethiopian giant executed for the entertainment of two Roman couples; Alex's assault of the Cat Lady in *Clockwork Orange*; Redmond's brawl with Toole at Dun Laoghaire's camp in *Barry Lyndon*.

At times, circularity seals fate: Alex walks around the circle line of the square prison yard, like a clockwork machine; Bowman and Poole are observed by HAL 9000, which reduces their space to the circle of its eye; space is reduced by Dax's binoculars focusing on the impossible target that is the Ant Hill, in *Paths of Glory*; the killer's kiss is accomplished with a rotational move of bodies in *Killer's Kiss*; the war room foreshadows the Doomsday shroud of the atomic mushroom in Dr. Strangelove; the razor's curve on the marines' heads anticipates the scythe-sweeping of the Vietnam war in *Full Metal Jacket*; Mrs. Haze's seduction rumba in her panther dress in front of Humbert discloses her hysteria; and, of course, the Kafkaian, Xanaduesque Overlook Hotel in *The Shining*, which Danny's round wheels drive pass, closely followed by the camera, to stop at room 237, the room of horrors.

The circular Odyssey of Kubrick's characters is complemented with another parameter: the maze of their exterior or interior universe, which equates in many aspects the circle figure, as Pierre Giuliani writes:

> The world is a circle, the absolute circle... The circular form, which the labyrinth attempts to merge with, is both the most and the least obsolete of models: it refers to its own re-beginning and its own extinction, both are never complete, ceaselessly receding. What moves apart repeats, what moves away returns. The circular labyrinth dominates the movement, or the agitation of the Kubrickian character, on moral as well as geographical and social levels. Everything concurs in ontology of fixedness, fatality and powerlessness. This is due to the crane shots, the

pan shots and the conflictual dolly in and dolly out which the eye memorizes as the Kubrickian signature and which outline the journey and its stagnation. Humbert Humbert, lost on the roads, on his hobbyhorse, returning incessantly to his starting point.[85]

Jack's chimera in *The Shining*, his obstinacy with writing, and the awareness of his incapacity to become the writer he has always wanted, open the door to his personal maze, within which he loses himself to no return - at least as a living human being.[86] Even if Danny returns as a new Theseus from the maze chase with his father, Daedalus-Jack is killed by his own Minotaur: his monstrous derangement, just like Humbert, Jack D. Ripper or even HAL 9000. Most of them lose their way in the labyrinth of their own conscience, transforming their Odyssey in a whirling, bewildering, impossible journey. As Michel Ciment observes:

> The labyrinth, both a spatial and temporal expression, seems to be the ideal place of completion of every Kubrickian voyage. If it is too - as Paolo Santarcangeli noticed - the symbol of the mother's womb, the intestines, it continues the objective correlate that the Overlook hotel already was in relation to Jack's psyche. Finally, combining two motifs linked to the infinite, but the first one: the closed, maleficent, pessimistic interlace - this the Eternal Return linked to Jack -

> the second: the open, positive, optimistic spiral - the perpetual becomingness linked to Danny.[87]

The Eternal Return which is once again related to the Odyssean theme is supplemented with the labyrinthic aspect of the Kubrickian Odysseus's peregrination, as Freddy Buache notes:

> The voyage's principal stages clearly draw this trajectory which runs from interstellar navigation to the horizon of Psyche. Eternal Return, one may say. Yes, but it is not just circular: it is rather a helicoid movement seen from a rear-view mirror in motion.[88]

But the intricacy of the maze's representation inaugurates a new dimension to the Kubrickian circular stylization, Buache's helicoid movement being cinematographically reproducible on rare occasions but closely related to a spiraling recurrence observable in the director's aestheticization of the Odyssean intermeshing.

Circle perfection for Kubrick seems unsatisfying if not too rigid in the depiction of Odysseus's journey: the sinuous line is a better achievement. The spiral is not a complete line nor a perfect circumference but a group of ever moving incomplete circumferences ascending towards perfection without turning away from it. It is the *je ne sais quoi* which, Georges Poulet writes, has no fixed form:

> It is the contrary of the circle, though it starts from the circle, returns to the circle, pretends to be not just a circle but myriad of circles. It is conceivable as a movement of both escape and return, as a capricious faithfulness to a model always loved and always forgotten. It is variety within unity and unity within variety.[89]

The sinuous line is before all, William Hogarth's creation, the S-shaped serpentine line that he describes in The Analysis of Beauty:

> The serpentine line, by its waving and winding at the same time different ways, leads the eye in a pleasing manner along the continuity of its variety, if I may be allowed the expression.

Kubrick's rendering of Hogarth is prevalent in most of his motion pictures[90]: in *Barry Lyndon*, Hogarth's technique is not only used with the truest fashion but his paintings[91] have deeply inspired the director-photographer.

From the zigzagging trenches of *Paths of Glory* to the sinuous roads of *Lolita*, from Alex's serpentine serpent in *Clockwork Orange* to the convoluting paths of Barry Lyndon, the Line of Beauty, as David Bindman writes, seizes Nature in its variety:

> The chief source of delight in nature is variety and this applies equally to a work of art. Intricacy of

effect is particularly pleasing, for it leads the eye's limited field of vision and the empathy between the eye's movement and the movement in nature; in Hogarth's simile an eye observing a dancing woman "was dancing with her all the time." Hogarth reduces these notions of variety and empathy to a basic line, a serpentine curve which can be observed equally in art and nature and is at the basis of all beautiful forms.[92]

To transcribe the S undulating motion in a cinematic language Kubrick follows or precedes his characters' advance with a tracking movement for which he is the most renown: in *Paths of Glory*, the camera dollies out on General Mireau and Lieutenant Roget, revealing the reality of the trenches and the tortuous closeness to death of their temporal inhabitants, for as Thomas Gray writes:

> The Boast of Heraldry, the pomp of Power, And all the beauty, all that Wealth e'er gave Awaits alike th'inevitable Hour. The Paths of Glory lead but to the Grave.[93]

The Paths of Glory are sinuous indeed, and the battleground shot by Kubrick presents a crooked, meandering topography - a surrealist graveyard[94] - which is opposed to the perpendicular geometry of the chateau. The soldiers are captured within the meandrous trenches as well as in the maze of the generals' personal ambition, their rotational movements when hit by a bullet lugubriously coinciding with the waltz of the officers during General Broulard's reception.

In *Clockwork Orange*, Alex's majestic zigzagging in the drugstore, accompanied by a winding movement of the camera, depicts the conquering personality of the character and his appropriation of space, though an impression of narrowing confinement foreshadows the prison episode. But more intriguing is the fabulous correspondence between this shot and Lord Bullingdon's as-majestic-entrance in Barry Lyndon's club, a temporal juxtaposition emerging from the flexuous connection, the dolly movement capturing in space and time the meandering Odysseus[95]. As Sandro Bernardi notes:

> The dolly movement follows a character in his progress and maintains him at the center of the frame. The movement is abolished or preserved; it is the shot of the absolute and decontextualized movement, the movement tends to immobility... Space stretches along a narrow, dark corridor, a tortuous path, a road which has - once run over again in the opposite way - neither destination nor direction, twisted and deviated to inevitably open out onto a reversed perspective, within a series by Hogarth - *The Rake's Progress* (1735).[96]

Barry Lyndon's sinuous Odyssey - prototypical of the picaresque Odyssey - terminates with a failure - appearing like the tragic flaw, the hamartia of the Kubrickian hero, like Jack's or Humbert's, leading them to their grave, or Dr. Harford's being spared his life by a prostitute - not because of the non-obtaining of the goal, as Georges Poulet writes, but because of the absence of any goal:

> The sinuous line goes nowhere. It is a hieroglyphic without meaning, a scribble, an elaborate but futile gesture. Unfaithful to the circle, erratic, supremely eccentric, it hampers itself in its own network, exhausted by the multiplicity of its tours and detours; it finishes by bisecting like a fatigued river to numb in some delta.[97]

Fatigued by his internal labyrinth, Jack numbs forever in the terminus of the Overlook Hotel's past. In *The Shining*, moreover, the use of the Steadycam allows spatial and motional prowess, especially in the Overlook Hotel's kitchen, where the camera dollies out in an undulating motion between the ovens, or during the maze chase.

The Handycam is also used masterfully in the capturing of sinuous eccentricities and disordered atmospheres: harmonious, symmetrical, rigorously framed shots are suddenly unbalanced by the movements of the Handycam. Bullingdon's interruption of the concert activates his fight with Barry on the ground. The order of Mr. Alexander's flat - the symmetry established by the mirrors and the checkered ground -, in *A Clockwork Orange* is followed by Alex's beating him and raping his wife. The

Handycam expresses the confusion of a mortal combat like no other camera and seizes movement in its most uncontrolled and uncontrollable aspect.

The Serpentine line is also the line of uncontrollable freedom, which consists in following one's whim and opting for the changing routes proposed by one's fancy, as is the case for Humbert, Alex, Barry, Jack, Joker, and Bill Harford. But Kubrick infers that the character's freedom is fatal to him: an unconscious or exterior factor - which, paradoxically, procured freedom - has associated it with madness, depredation and self-delusion. As Georges Poulet writes:

> If I am free to follow the curve of my fancy, this very fancy is predetermined by a whole mechanism of external and internal laws. The sinuosity of my thought depends of the exterior conditions which surround me, the sensitive experiences which modify me and finally, the law of association of my ideas... which insidiously constrain it to pass from one idea to the other as one passes from a concave to a convex curve at the point of coincidence.[98]

The sinuous line is the symbol of Nature and life, but it is also a feminist symbol: the line of beauty for Humbert Humbert is certainly Lolita's wavy shape, which waves incessantly in his fantasy and conducts his straight

55 *Stanley Kubrick: The Odysseys*

Odyssey into a torturous peregrination. The shapes of naked women in *Eyes Wide Shut* embark Dr. Harford in a dream-like, sexual odyssey during which he infiltrates a massive masked orgy of an unnamed secret society, pushed by his own jealous flashbacks in which he enacts his wife's sexual dream.

To a certain extent, women are always meditative within the masculine Odyssey: Eve, Dalila, Circe, Penelope. In *Killer's Kiss*, Davy falls in love with Gloria and enters the underworld of Vinnie Rapallo, Gloria's crooked lover, which he has to kill.[99] In *The Killing*, most male characters are implicated in a hold-up for the love of their wives or mistresses. The best example is Sherry, for whom George risks his job, freedom and life. She sabotages the plan by involving her young lover, Val, into it and causes the loss of all, even of her own life. In *Barry Lyndon*, Redmond challenges Captain Quin to a duel - thus activating his Odyssey - because of Nora, his beloved cousin, who accepted Quin's proposal of marriage. Another woman - Lady Lyndon - induces his ascent as well as his descent. In *Spartacus*, Varinia is coveted by the rivals Crassus and Gracchus, but remains faithful to Spartacus, like Penelope to Odysseus. In *Paths of Glory*, a young German woman brings tears to the eyes of the ruthless French soldiers by singing a German song. So does a young Viet Cong woman to the ruthless Marines, but by shooting them, in *Full Metal Jacket*. Alice Harford's dream triggers her husband's sexual odyssey in *Eyes Wide Shut*.

In *A Clockwork Orange*, the Cat Lady alerts the Police before Alex kills her and is arrested. Moreover, the Ludovico technique he is submitted to annihilates his masculine attraction towards the sinuous silhouette of women. And, finally, Wendy, Jack's Penelope, whom he truly, madly, cannibalistically loves to the point of wanting to cut her into pieces. The line of beauty in Kubrick reveals the hero's incapacity to master his destiny, parallel to his captivity within the circular mechanism of the Odyssey.

Kubrick's Odysseus appears to be a prisoner of his own fate, however free his sinuous Odyssey might appear. As for the Eternal Return, superior forces are at work on him, like Poseidon's whimsical blowing on the girouette-like Odysseus. In Kubrick, the Return of Odysseus turns the man of many turns in an ever-turning top. Unsurprisingly, each of Kubrick's characters are confronted with dizziness, as each film is faced with muddled tracks and proposes a new angle of view, both reversed and returned, to the spectator, however constraining this may be. The return of Odysseus equates Kubrick's returning cinema as well as his torsion of our vision.

The Odyssey of Moonwatcher

From the caves of the Pleistocene era to the intergalactic expanses of the third millenary, from a closed world to an infinite universe,[100] the Odyssey of Moonwatcher is also our own. From our cavernous movie theatres to the Kubrickian universe, our Odyssey as watchers-spectators accomplishes a similar metamorphic ascent towards cinematographic infinity, the quadrilateral screen-shaped monolith being a catalyst agent intervening in our cinematic evolution, as it did for Moonwatcher. As the monolith works within the subconscious of Moonwatcher[101] to activate his first steps towards progress, so does the monolith-screen within ours, especially with *2001*, which is, as Kubrick declared, "a visual experience."[102]

One that bypasses verbalized pigeonholing and directly penetrates the subconscious with an emotional and philosophical content. The film is an intensely subjective experience that reaches the viewer at an inner level of consciousness. You are free to speculate as you wish about the philosophical and allegorical meaning of the film - and such speculation is one indication that it has succeeded in gripping the audience at a deep level.[103]

A Clockwork Orange, which succeeds *2001*, discusses the theme of mental conditioning through pictures - the Ludovico technique, Alex being like a Platonician caveman chained to his seat, watching the shadows of reality[104] projected on the cave's wall. The Kubrick Technique - through its work on inner consciousness and its use of slow pacing, hypnotic, songs-of-sirens-like soundtracks - seems to mesmerize[105] its patient and prepare him for an Odyssey beyond Jupiter, beyond the bounds of cinema, beyond his own perceptive bonds. As Dudley Andrew writes:

> Beneath such concepts as the limitation of perception and the integrity of space lies a belief in the signifying power of nature. When a filmmaker puts a situation under the pressure of a controlled gaze, he forces it to reveal its structural depth, to bring out the preexisting relations.[10]

A journey through the Kubrickian universe is inevitably traumatizing for the Moonwatcher-spectator, who is submitted to a kinesthetic, psychological manipulation which increases his passivity. He is suddenly launched in an interpretational vacuum, in which he plunges in quest for the sense, an active - and retroactive - combat against the semantic aphasia, the meaningful hiatus which results from the iconographic void expressed by the "ambush-shots":

- o the 18th century room, the Star-Child,
- o the monolith, the 1921 picture of *The Shining*,
- o the opening of Jack's food-safe jail,
- o Jack's look over - if not Over-look - the miniature maze,
- o the Victorian love scene concluding *Clockwork Orange*,
- o *Barry Lyndon*'s photogrammic immobilization;
- o *Eyes Wide Shut*, a code among occult societies signifying either that someone is close minded or that he or she should keep their eyes closed (and mouth shut) in front of a misdeed.

All these are part of Kubrick's entrapping symbolization destined to act and react upon the active Moonwatcher. As Thierry Cazals notes:

> Systematically organizing the space of the seeing, the director manipulates signs rather than bodies. This work on the seeing, this explosion-implosion of the referential, makes cinema no longer a primitive art but a reflective.[107]

Our unanswered, multi-conceptual, multidirectional questioning developed earlier in this book helped us frame *2001*'s reflective scope, concluding that the film's true meaning is found beyond the myriad of interpretations it has produced.

To analyze the Kubrick Technique in depth, the screen-like monolith is the perfect example. For if one examines the constellation of possible explanations, one may feel in front of a Kubrickian amphibology.[108] A simple, black stone can become:

- the plinths of Stonehenge;
- the Cyclopean statuary of Easter Island;
- the black stone of the Mecca;
- Ernst Fuchs's creations;
- the symbol of the unknowable; of supreme wisdom; of knowledge,
- the Tree of Knowledge;
- the symbol of mathematical purity;
- of God,[109] of course, but God, as Freddy Buache writes, is an all-purpose word turning eventually into a trap or a mask;
- the Mosaic tablets;
- a druidical stone;
- the manifest sentinel[110] of the extraterrestrial intelligence that existed four million years ago;
- a place of perdition;
- a divine gift;
- a cosmic and cerebral ruler, as Gilles Deleuze writes;[111]

- an emblem, more than an artifact, of the Mystery Beyond;
- a mirror;
- a door;[112]
- a Rorschach test,
- a closed window on the world, Magritte's windows.

Magritte's windows, which as Sandro Bernardi writes, only open on another image: "Kubrick is the director who introduced the largest symbolical manifestation in movie making, by condensing and over-determining in a single object all the possibilities contained in the visible. The image of the black monolith, the mirror-object which engenders so many questionings but transforms the spectators into interpreters, the image of the pure possibility of the unlimited opening of the sense."[113]

Kubrick transforms his Moonwatchers into hermeneutists, but also establishes the new frontiers of cinema[114], these are Kubrick's cinematographic objectives. But to reach these stages, Kubrick must lure his audiences into allegorical ambushes, leading them into an Odyssey of the sign - but without a map, as Sandro Bernardi writes:

> How can we cross this field riddled with metaphorical traps, hidden circularities, tautological discoveries? A field looking like Madeleine de Scudéry's "map of Tendre" drawn a

long time ago, in which the directions were missing: the metaphorical traveler, when he did not lose himself in the different forms of passion could only arrive at his starting point.[115]

This Odyssey, however, can soon become our maze, within which our receptivity - like Jack's - freezes and dies of analytical exhaustion.[116] The exit is to be found within our decoding methods and automatisms which confine us, often, to our interpretative caves - "inside a film artist's cave." As T.A. Nelson noticed about The Shining:

> Kubrick deliberately - some say perversely - gives and takes away at the same time. But, aesthetically, the maze concept requires that an audience be tested and challenged, even to the point of confusion if it fails to shine and remember not only how it got into the film (i.e., the guided tours of narrative exposition) but how it got lost. In retracing those steps, the viewer might discover that it wasn't Kubrick's *The Shining* that betrayed him but all those false expectations that tyrannize audiences into believing that filmic understandings should follow straight paths into a center of meaning.[117]

Moreover, his technique seems to lobotomize our spectatorial idiosyncrasies. Like Bowman in HAL's mechanical brain - Kubrick seems to be combatting the one-eyed, Cyclops-like spectator.

Similarly, he seems to be dislocating our musical apprehension by using György Ligeti's dissonant, disturbing melodies, the experience being visual and auditory, destructive[118] and constructive. Kubrick's technique cultivates our stereotyping propensities, by proposing us déjà vu films, dealing with broadly adapted stories: Vietnam war, haunted house, E.T. encounter, hold-up, to systematically dynamite the narrative structure of the subject treated. As Thierry Cazals writes:

> Starting from the structures of classical narration - succession of adventures, of epochs, of dramatic ascent and denouement - he then abandons his movies to their deprograming and incompletion. Rigid frames dynamited from inside, continuations as scale model.[119]

There is in Kubrick a constant reference to the cinematographic memory manifested in a permanent borrowing of genre movies and literature. As Pierre Giuliani writes, newness is engendered by the destruction of ancientness. An extra-referential system seems to connect Kubrick's films to their cinematographic antecedents, the spectator's Odyssey passing through a series of familiar pictures before returning to the film and the new texture it proposes.

For instance, *The Killing* is a voyage through film noir and gangster literature - the scenario being an adaptation of Lionel White's *Clean Break* - directly connected with John Huston's *The Asphalt Jungle* (in which Sterling Hayden plays), also centered around hoodlums and horseraces and Howard Hawks's *The Big Sleep* (in which Elisha Cook plays a miserable hood manipulated by a vicious woman), or again Huston's *The Maltese Falcon* (still with Elisha Cook). By utilizing this referential package Kubrick maps a route[120] for the spectator which he inevitably re-configurates after the exposition scenes.

The Killing introduces a horizontal, typical development which is soon questioned, regulated and, subsequently, elaborated within an involute, rhapsodic formula, which invigorates the former structure and conducts the genre and the traveler-spectators towards new possibilities. It is similar for science-fiction or historical movies, horror or war movies. This iconoclastic approach has become Kubrick's modus operandi resulting in deep innovations which have had a momentous influence on the succeeding generations of directors. *2001*'s multidirectional departure, for instance, revolutionized Science-Fiction movies, there was to be a "before" and an "after" *2001*.

The Shining is the implosive criticism of occult films - an internal analysis of the genre as well as its literature - Stephen King's best-seller being "passed through the screen." References to former creations are also effected, a whole fantastic historicism[121] taking place in *The Shining*: *The Exorcist* for Danny and his possessed finger; *Psycho* for "Arbogast/Jack" and his axe; John Cassavetes's *A Woman Under the Influence* for Wendy's hysteria; Franz Kafka's style and castle for the Overlook Hotel - twin brother to Charles Foster Kane's; plus an indirect reference to F. W. Murnau; but, more to the point, a direct reference to the 1970's fondness for trashy, B-Grade, zombiesque movies, which Kubrick wants to exterminate.

Kubrick, once again, starts from the classical structures of his subject, which he subtly disconnects: the Kubrickian ellipsis is in function quite early in the movie - Danny's premonitions and hallucinations - rapidly perforating the spectator's normative decoding process. It has been said that Kubrick is unwilling to spill blood - gore is not always funny - and the non-sequiturs of dark verbal slapstick suffice. He concentrates his energy on the mystery effect - dear to Stephen King:

> The only law of the genre is that you must not try to explain or find clear explanations to what happens, the whole meaning is to produce an impression of strangeness on the audience. H. P. Lovecraft said that you should never try and explain what happens as long as it stimulates the people's imagination and their sense of strangeness, of anxiety and of fear.[122]

Kubrick introduced new dimensions to the genre, not only by exploring the field of strangeness[123] in depth, but by associating it with Sigmund Freud's essay, *The Uncanny*. The film's psychological basis: especially when the symbolical fusion between Jack's madness and the Overlook Hotel is attained. Moreover, his co-writing of the script with Diane Johnson, a professor in Gothic literature permitted him to introduce a mythical inscription [124] inferred by the labyrinth which is not found in Stephen King's novel.

Applying his deconstructive if not deconstructionist formula to his new object of study: war film, in *Full Metal Jacket*, [125] Kubrick attempts to exorcize the way Vietnam haunts over the American audience - somewhat in accordance with Francis Ford Coppola's *Apocalypse Now*. He declared in *Newsweek* that he wanted to make the narrative structure of *Full Metal Jacket* [126] burst, which is also true for the Vietnam war stereotypes and clichés or any other propagandist pictures which have conditioned the spectator to a point of no return, all established by a list stretching from John Wayne's *The Green Berets* to George Cosmatos's *Rambo* and Michael Cimino's *The Deer Hunter*. Repelling the traditional, Hollywood Manichaeism of war and the American myth of the indestructible hero fighting against the evil forces "to protect freedom and democracy," Kubrick focuses on antiheroes who are vaguely intellectual and stubborn or bulimic and simple-minded, mostly torn between the crushing mechanism of war and a basic incomprehension of the situation they are in.

The subject of war is not new to Kubrick, and its content is rather situated in the continuity of his early reflections: the dualism of *Fear and Desire*, the pamphleteer pacifism of *Paths of Glory*, the satirical catastrophism of *Dr. Strangelove*, the irony of *Barry Lyndon*, or Bill Harford's harrowing and perilous nightlong odyssey of moral and sexual discovery which he hardly comprehends in *Eyes Wide Shut*.

Furthermore, there is a general sense of anti-militarism and anti-Americanism of most of his films. *Full Metal Jacket* is a criticism of war pictures and consequently boycotts war pictures: the only fight appearing to be against an invisible enemy, a monolith-like, Overlook-like building[127] on which marines are thrown and crushed like clockwork oranges. The apex of irony: the invisible enemy is a woman - the spitting image of Wendy - which is executed like an animal. Absence being a modality of presence, the absence of war pictures in the film has for only purpose to underline the global, real censure imposed on Vietnam. Besides, the second part of the film is more concerned with the image of war than war itself, Lieutenant Lockart, of *Stars and Stripes*, the army's paper, symbolizing the controlled filtering of information and images.

Kubrick's camera - shooting the army's camera shooting the boys - penetrates a Kubrickian fourth dimension equating the 18th-century room or the 1921 photograph, it is the dimension of reality and fiction, as Pierre Giuliani writes:

> When the film's cameras shoot the television's, war is suddenly sandwiched between the pictures made by war - through television - and those invented by war - through cinema. An absolutely discomforting situation, which only a moral rearmament movie could contest if not contradict.[128]

The extra-referential factor is omnipresent in Kubrick and participates in the repulsing of cinema's as well as the spectator's limits. It is present in *Clockwork Orange*[129] and Alex's visions, which are, as Michel Ciment writes, fed by Hollywood: Alex projects himself into Dracula, in a centurion whipping Christ, in an oriental prince enjoying the pleasures of the flesh, as in Cecil B. De Mille's ancient movies or even Kubrick's *Spartacus*.[130] Alex is also conditioned by American action movies and Nazi propagandist pictures, violence being somehow engendered and abolished through pictures. The referential factor is also present in *Lolita*'s disrupting of the American moral codes which succeeds very closely Luis Buñuel's *La niña*.[131]

There is a persistent questioning of forms in Kubrick, a criticism of filmic production but, above all, a quest - Odyssean perhaps - for improvement issued from the confrontation of ancient and modernist styles which inscribes his work at the borderline of classic and contemporary creations,[132] thus allowing him a broader audience.[133] As Sandro Bernardi notes:

> Kubrick's lifework - always torn between a classical narrative tendency (which makes it pleasant and acceptable for the traditional spectator used to an anthropocentric representation) and avant-garde, experimental cinema (which tends to shatter representation) is ideal to underline the double tendency of cinema to use pictures as instruments of discourse and narration and, inversely, forget the meaning, in reporting on the picture all the representative activity. Divided between the poetical tendency of modern cinema - Antonioni, Wenders, Tarkovsky, Godard - and the reverse tendency of narrative cinema - with this cinematographic conscience which is found in Coppola, Scorsese, Demme.[134]

Responding symmetrically to this extra-referential system projected on the unconscious screen of the spectator-traveler, the intra-referential organization renders him even more active in his Odyssey through the Kubrickian universe.

Furthermore, if there is a complex network of correspondence between the Kubrickian body and the others, there is an even more complex, organismic[135] connection between each cellular, microcosmic creation which composes the body of his lifework. As T.A. Nelson writes:

> Kubrick's film universe before *2001* thrives on associations and connections, no matter how paradoxical or surreal, and the workings of separate elements within larger and more ambiguous wholes.[136]

The Kubrickian Odyssey is based on an involute structure which refers and returns constantly to its components, each microcosmic Odyssey continuing the preceding Odysseys through a filial perpetuation or being continued by the succeeding, in a unifying, dynamic, vivacious process.

Like the extra-referential system, there are two types of intra-references: direct references which explicitly connect one film to another and indirect, implicit references, in other words, stylistic recurrences which establish a global cohesion. Direct references are usually found in the chronologically dovetailing films, as may be observed between: Alex's look- during *Clockwork Orange*'s first shot - and the Star-Child's - during *2001*'s last; *Dr. Strangelove*'s atomic mushroom accompanied by the song "We'll meet again ... some sunny day" and *2001*'s first shot on the sun plus its deserted, post-Apocalyptic landscape; Jack's grin on the picture and the marines' when being skin-headed.

References may also appear almost inadvertently during the film's development: in *Lolita*, Quilty, covered with a toga-like sheet, declares to Humbert: "I am Spartacus"[137], Barry Lyndon buys a painting by Ludovico, recalling Alex's Ludovico technique in *Clockwork Orange*. Linking *Clockwork Orange* to *2001*, the tramp, being beaten by Alex and his droogs, declares that:

> It's a stinking world...Men on the moon and men spinning around the earth and there's not no attention paid to earthly law and order no more.[138]

The implicit references are multiple and may be gathered under common factors: The close-up on the eyes all underlying the character's rage or fear:[139]

- Moonwatcher in the cave,
- Bowman in the space-pod,
- the Star-child,
- Alex in the Korova Milkbar,
- frozen Jack, telepathic Danny,
- Pyle before his suicide in *Full Metal Jacket*.

The scenes of the beating up with a peculiar thudding common to all and a sense of unchanged brutality in man:

- Spartacus and the slave on a Roman senator,
- Moonwatcher and his clan, using the bone-weapon for the first time,
- Alex and his droogs on the tramp,
- Joker and the marines[140], using the toweled-soap-weapon on Pyle.

The high and low angles on the stairs:

- Davy and Gloria climbing the stairs to Vinnie Rapallo's club and the ominous inscription, *watch your step*;
- Humbert's climbing after Quilty,
- Jack's climbing after Wendy,

The last two underlying the analogy between Humbert's derangement and Jack's madness.

- The axe: Jack's and Vinnie Rapallo's.
- The boxing,
- The duels,
- The wheelchairs,
- The chessboards,

- The billiard tables,
- The bathrooms...

All these elements are important in Kubrick's oeuvre, they cultivate the spectator's tendency to merge the parts to the whole.

Other correlations also contribute to this unification and allow us to encircle Kubrick's themes of predilection. Victims and victimizers, for instance, are recurrently obsessional:

- Spartacus and Batianus,
- Colonel Dax and General Mireau,
- Humbert and Quilty,
- Bowman and HAL,
- Alex and the warder in chief,
- Barry and Captain Potzdorf,
- Private Pyle and Sergeant Hartman.
- Dr. Bill Harford and the secret society

The Kubrickian universe seems to be constituted of two types of individuals, the oppressor and the oppressed, the relationship between the two introducing tensions, conflicts or rebellions.

In addition, the various topics appear to respond to one another: the technique used to kill the criminal reflex in

Clockwork Orange is counterbalanced by the method employed to raise the killing instincts in *Full Metal Jacket*. Alex's concluding words: "I was cured all right" and Joker's "I am alive and I am not afraid," accentuating the parallelism [141]; Marcellus in *Spartacus* "likes to kill for the example", like General Mireau in *Paths of Glory*; Gracchus and Crassus use people like pawns for their own promotion, like Broulard and Mireau; dreaming Alex sees himself as an Oriental lover conquering the hearts of his wife's servants, as Barry does with Lady Lyndon's servants; Alex is "reformed" as Bowman is transformed.

The correspondences are innumerable in Kubrick, a unifying inclination resulting from the referential bridges projected between each movie. The spectator-traveler - when watching a Kubrick film - is actually watching several, he is even taking part in a thematic dialectics which associates and dissociates concepts and forms, which questions, answers and questions again, follows a thesis-antithesis process, proposes films and their contraries: opting for sex and ultra-violence in *Clockwork Orange*; and a more decent line of conduct as in *Barry Lyndon*, in which the 18th century's libertine atmosphere is only whispered; or the society's producing of killing machine in *Full Metal Jacket* opposing the subject of violence control in *Clockwork Orange* once again through mechanism, treating outer space in *2001* and inner in *The*

Shining, secret society and high society in *Eyes Wide Shut.*

But these apparent, thematic contradictions represent the artist's attempt to seize the world. His alternating between past and future, Earth or space, Europe or United States has for only function to comment on the present fractures[142] of modern society, which splits man in two, dualism equating schizophrenia in Kubrick, the modern Odysseus looking like a dissolute being, oppressed by exterior mechanisms, lost in the maze of dehumanizing modernity. The structural unity of his filmic universe might therefore appear like the artist's quest for self-preservation, his Zarathustresque cave, similar to his London residence which he barely ever left, his 18th-century room.[143]

One may speak of a protective womb that the artist established for himself against the immensity of the universe, a meaningful attempt to recreate harmony against the meaninglessness of the outside world, a harmonious universe replacing the celestial spheres by musical, circular films. Not with a view to creating a superior - elitist - race of spectators, like Dr. Strangelove's eugenic plan under the mines' shaft, but the need to transport as many spectators as possible through the cathartic depiction[144] of a contingent universe.[145]

Kubrick's life-time achievement is a mirror-monolith which transcends Moonwatcher into a child-like spectator, cleansed of prejudices and preconditioning. The Odyssey beyond Jupiter, beyond the spectators' possibilities, is achieved through reflection, mirrors being present at every stage of the Kubrickian journey as well as replication, doubles and symmetries. They reveal, as Pierre Giuliani writes, the duality of the world and the way to death.[146]

In *Killer's Kiss*, for instance, mirrors exhibit Gloria and show Davy's voyeurism simultaneously as the camera - placed in a strategic position in which both front and rear can be seen - captures both scenes in the same shot. [147] Mirrors also unveil Vinnie Rapallo's gnawing jealousy as he burst in anger at his own reflection [148] and throws his glass on it. In *Dr. Strangelove*, the mirror doubles the space of General Buck Turgidson's civil room, as opposed to the three military places of the movie. In *The Shining*, the mirror betrays Jack's distress - like M in a shop window.[149] In *Clockwork Orange*, it symmetrizes space, as in Mr. Alexander's entrance hall - similarly to the plot's symmetry: Alexander is also Alex's double[150] but more interesting is Thomas Allen Nelson's remark:

> Alex is a victim of an institutional monolith - state, church, science - that would deprive him of his visions - of violence and beauty - by transforming him into the ultimate Clockwork-

> Man, a two-way-mirror, at once an object for others to contemplate and a voyeur.[151]

In *Barry Lyndon*, Lady Lyndon's servant reads a French poem describing the reflection of light on loving beings;[152] in *Lolita*, Quilty acts as Humbert Humbert's Doppelgänger,[153] Humbert being already double by his name; in *2001*, Poole and Bowman represent mirror twins more than true doubles, especially after it becomes apparent that a computer, not Poole, will play Quilty to Bowman's Humbert.

Not only does Kubrick choose two actors with significant physical resemblances, but he repeatedly places them in visual or comparative contexts that create a mirroring effect. In most two-shots Bowman occupies screen right and Poole screen left, while in one-shots an empty space or chair recalls the missing twin. In *Fear and Desire*, the theme of the double is already treated, as two characters are played by the same actor[154], a fact which obviously recalls Peter Sellers and his multiple characters in *Lolita* and *Dr. Strangelove*.

But the theme was also present in *Day of the Fight*,[155] which shares twenty-four hours with Walter Cartier, the boxer, before his match. As Sandro Bernardi noticed, Cartier is shot with his twin brother who never leaves him. In *Spartacus*, a hundred slaves stand up to the name of Spartacus; HAL is confronted to his double on earth in

2001; Danny's psychological need is to create an internal double to protect himself against the unexplained visions he has and also against his father, who maltreated him when he was three, his schizophrenia leading him to mirror writing and redrum for murder.

Moreover, *2001* is *Dr Strangelove*'s philosophical mirror, as T.A. Nelson infers: "a Kubrickian mirror that reflects a positive harmony of form and substance rather than a madness in the disguise of beauty."[156] Each film seems to be a mirror plate fitting in the frame of Kubrick's lifework held at the world: a distorted mirror which, instead of being truly reflective, is doubtlessly reflective, if not introspective on the audience.

In distortion, reality is observable, as Kubrick's new amphibology infers. The distortion of pictures, as in *2001* or even in *Killer's Kiss*, where pictures are deformed to return to an original flashing form of light and of negatives, or in *Clockwork Orange*, where images are accelerated or slowed down ad libitum, and where colors attack the eye barbarously, deliberately; or again in *Barry Lyndon*, where pictures tend to pictorialism and a return to painting and fixity: in Kubrick, distorted pictures and mirrors reveal the hidden face of the world.

Stanley Kubrick: The Odysseys

Distortion in Kubrick is adjacent to dissolution: dissolution of meaning and of forms but also of beings or groups of beings, cells which are eliminated or rejected from the body.[157] *Full Metal Jacket* shows a cellular universe which is soon disrupted, as is the case in the cell-like American family of *The Shining*, or in *Barry Lyndon*'s 18th century on the verge of destruction.[158] As Michel Ciment writes:

> Each of his movies is the story of a disintegration, a breaking apart. Most of times, a group slowly dissolves, loses each of its members - *Fear and Desire*, *The Killing*, *Paths of Glory*, *Spartacus*, *2001*, *Clockwork Orange*, *Full Metal Jacket* - or the familial cell, or even the couple, disintegrate - *Lolita*, *Barry Lyndon*, *The Shining* - without omitting the very body of these characters which are mutilated, amputated, wounded.[159]

Inevitable fragmentation of the body, the corpse, the Marines' corpse, in which the cells are promised a simulacrum of immortality–as Sergeant Hartman yells: "the marines die, the corpse lives forever."

Fragmentation is omnipresent in *Clockwork Orange* as Alex's dystopian society appears like morsel clans, which integrate, disintegrate or reject: the droogs, Alex's family, the police, the church, the politicians, the scientists, all ruled by proper social, moral, even linguistic codes. Alex and his droogs, for instance, speak a jargon, the Nadsat which is a mixture of English and Slavic of Burgessian origin[160] and which protects the group and differentiates it from the others.

The general discrepancies and the problematic incommunicability separating each antagonist cell are generative of tensions and cellular frictions and, consequently, of violence or ultra-violence. This astrictive interaction of autarkic cells, clans, groups, and corpses stems from a problem of communication and language, made paroxysmal by Kubrick and his underlying point that language is used both as a tool and as a weapon.[161]

The subject is not new to Kubrick, *Dr. Strangelove* and *2001* show characters living in closed worlds, isolated in alveolus which do not communicate, using a language proper to the cell: the simians' gibberish was their only weapon until they replaced it by a bone, HAL's tech-nish[162] is associated with his hypnotic, ominous tone, the monolith's shrills destabilize the boastful scientists, the same scientist's strangulating jargon is counterbalanced by banalities, the Russians' politely repetitive questions are offered a politely repetitive, robotic answer from Dr. Floyd: "this is top secret." In *Dr. Strangelove*, Ambassador de Sadesky's Russian opposes the military codification, the "code prefix plan R" engages the nuclear mechanism, General Jack D. Ripper's disconnected speech about "precious bodily fluids" turns the Army to ridicule.

These linguistic incoherencies are enhanced by the generalized interferences and uncommunicative relations that 2001's and Dr. Strangelove's universe are submitted to: silence is what HAL produces when Bowman asks for the opening of the airlock's door, the only possible access when knowing his situation outside in space. Consequently, Bowman penetrates HAL's brain to disconnect it, and HAL's speech slowly regresses to its robotic childhood as the song he renders proves.

HAL lip-reads Bowman and Poole's silent discussion in the pod and silence is Bowman's due in the white room. In Dr. Strangelove, transmissions are cut between the B52 and the base, communications are dead between the war room and the base, from his bathroom General Turgidson is shouted the content of the war-room's message by his playmate-secretary, and the shutters are down in Ripper's office as the base is made insular. Similarly insular is the Russian nuclear base of Laputa, which recalls Jonathan Swift's *Gulliver's Travels*, where Laputa is a flying island visited by Gulliver after his peregrination in the Giant's country: this island is peopled by astronauts who only communicate through geometric or musical relationships and who are addicted to visionary projects. Insular again is Parris Island in *Full Metal Jacket*, which is organized, as Bill Krohn writes:

> Like a brain composed of human cells which think and react the same way, until its functioning disintegrates: from inside, when a single cell - Pyle - begins to put the killer instinct directives into execution, then from outside, by the Têt onslaught which is the exteriorized representation of an identical force.[163]

In *Full Metal Jacket*, language is submitted to a military codification which intensifies the soldiers' cellularity,[164] their extraneousness culminating in their dehumanized nicknaming one another, a new identity which is soon to be pounded over by Sergeant Hartman's barbarous, scurrilous, scatological delivery.[165]

Cellularity is also observable in *The Shining*, in which three specimens of a same civilization are on board of a ghost ship, as the astronauts of *2001* were, and in which communication has become telepathic, spiritualistic, or disjointed, surpassing language, interfering beyond language and its verbal correlatives, invocative rather than evocative, as Jack's decontextualized parody of three little pigs, or his "here's Johnny": as signs of his crossing the line, his trespassing the line-space separating his repeated "all work and no play", his disarticulate manipulating of language which disarticulates him. There is a language regression in most of Kubrick's films, as Thierry Cazals writes:

> In Kubrick, there is explicitly this will to return to a pre-verbal cinema, thus to go beyond or under the psychological subject, to rediscover our unvoiced animosity, find our cosmic roots, the Kubrickian anti-hero are before all traversed by forces which are beyond them or by silent impulses. Twelve films, twelve regressions of speech, implacable deprograming of language: HAL's return to childhood, Sergeant Hartman's rude delivery, Clare Quilty's incoherent monologues, Alex's tribal codes, the apes' cries or Bowman's breathing. [166]

Language in Kubrick is also concerned with sexuality. *Lolita* and *Dr. Strangelove* emblematize the subtle manipulation of connotative speech, risqué puns, double-entendres, pushing language to the limits of a sexual entanglement[167], a necessary subterfuge against the pressures from the Production Code and the Catholic Legion of Decency.[168]

More flagrant is the denomination of places or people: Mr. Swine is the receptionist of the Enchanted Hunters Hotel, Lolita is sent to Camp Climax for the summer, a Rabelaisian technique developed to unimagined limits in *Dr. Strangelove*[169] :

- General Jack D. Ripper - after the famous ripper;
- Ambassador de Sadesky - after the Marquis;

- the Russian premier Kissoff;
- President Merkin Muffley[170];
- the bombs, which Major T.J. "King" Kong strides, are gargantuan phallus, which have been given sexually suggestive salutations: "Hi, there", "Dear, John";
- the Russian base of Laputa;
- General Buck Turgidson's turning simple sentences into sexual poetry: destroying the Russians becomes "catching them with their pants down."

In *Clockwork Orange* and *Full Metal Jacket*, sex is verbally ritualized–as in Alex's "old in-out, in-out"[171]–and it is – as in the Marines' love-making with their rifles ("this is my rifle, this is my gun"). Weapons are associated with women for the Marines and, symbolically, Alex kills the Cat Lady with an enormous phallus. In contrast, sexual discourse in *Eyes Wide Shut* is an ultimate statement. The movie oscillates between marriage and adultery while exploring the tension between love and desire, reality and fantasies, secret societies and the occult. "Fuck" is Nicole Kidman's last word in the movie's final scene. It is also the last word of Kubrick's last film. [172]

Language is negated in Kubrick, first by the narrator, and then by the director. The Kubrickian narrator is omniscient: Davy in *Killer's Kiss*, Johnny Clay in *The Killing*, Humbert, Alex, Joker, all relating their adventures with detachment, and reducing explanatory dialogues or heavy introduction to the essentials. Voice-over narrators are also present as in *Spartacus*, *Dr. Strangelove* and *Barry Lyndon*, the latter conflicting with his own narrative, as he ironically anticipates and reveals the action to come as little Brian's death, for instance, a revelation which intensifies the tragic scene. Similarly, the black boards introducing both parts of the film and concluding it inform the spectator of what he is going to see or what he has seen, a device borrowed from silent movies used in *2001* and *The Shining*. Silence, absence of language or drastic diminution of words are signs of Kubrick's absolute negation of language and his genuine wish to return to silent films.

In *Barry Lyndon*, the seduction scene between Barry and Lady Lyndon is only visual and brilliantly shot, emotions being conveyed and words are surpassed by the images. As in *2001*, where language negation reduces dialogues to one fourth of the running time. A meaningful look is what Bowman leaves us, and what Kubrick tells us. "Words, words, words", Hamlet said. Words are unnecessary, silent films are emotionally, interpretatively, visually unlimited. The vision is everything. Is it a return to silent films? Is this the meaning of Kubrick's Odyssey, a return to the primal, nascent form of cinema after an Odyssey through colors, sounds and innovations?

Fabrice Jaumont 86

Ithaca

Kubrick's unweaving and re-weaving of the cinematographic tapestry reflect his attachment to the changeability implied in the Odyssean theme, which has become the theme of perpetual questioning of one's possibilities. The camera's shuttling back and forth in time, round and round in space, through the means of dolly movements, shots and reverse shots, circular and spiraling recurrences, equates the director's shuttling between classical and avant-garde techniques, between painting and photography, between musical intensity and spatial silence. A chassé-croisé which the pluricephal director utilizes with a view to producing new angles of view and new parallaxes: a constant Kubrickian experimentation of the cinematographic language.

Kubrick's attempt to delineate the modern Odysseus and the revolutions he effectuates in his universe inevitably leads him to seize the tensions and frictions of the modern environment. Kubrick's contemporary Odysseus is a fractured man scattering in a distorted world and losing himself in the labyrinth of his meaningless and misunderstood Odyssey, turning and turning like a mechanical swimmer in a dehumanizing system.

But hope is to be found in the cathartic effect of cinema, in the metamorphoses occasioned by the Kubrickian Odyssey, which carries the spectator away from his cave of visual conditioning and prejudices and transports him through a field of flashing lights, "over an abyss, a dangerous crossing, a dangerous path, a dangerous looking back, a dangerous shudder and stop", to return him/her as a Star-Child, to "innocence and forgetfulness, a new beginning, a game, a wheel turning on itself, a first movement, a sacred yes", to Ithaca, the renascent state of cinema, in an Odyssey through film making, an Odyssey through film watching, the Odysseys of Stanley Kubrick.

Stanley Kubrick: Filmography

Director, Screenwriter, Producer, Director of Photography

Short films
- 1951   Day of the Fight
- 1951   Flying Padre
- 1953   The Seafarers

Feature films
- 1953   Fear and Desire
- 1955   Killer's Kiss
- 1956   The Killing
- 1957   Paths of Glory
- 1960   Spartacus
- 1962   Lolita
- 1964   Dr. Strangelove
- 1968   2001: A Space Odyssey
- 1971   A Clockwork Orange
- 1975   Barry Lyndon
- 1980   The Shining
- 1987   Full Metal Jacket
- 1999   Eyes Wide Shut

Notes

[1] See W.B Stanford, *The Ulysses Theme*.

[2] Webster's Third New International Dictionary, p 1564-1565

[3] W.B Stanford, *The Ulysses Theme*, p 4

[4] See Stanford p 324 - 327, for representations of Ulysses in the visual arts.

[5] The Homeric hero was played by Kirk Douglas. Halliwell's film guide writes: "peripatetic adventure yarn not too far after Homer, narrative style uncertain but highlights good." p1064

[6] Strick's Ulysses "had much charm and imagination though its faithful retention of Joyce's language caused it to be banned in many areas." Halliwell's Filmgoer's companion, p 794

[7] Which Kubrick called: "a mythological documentary"

[8] See Antoninus 's song in Kubrick's *Spartacus*: ."..and the twilight touches the shape of the wandering Earth, I turn home, through blue shadows of purple woods, I turn home, I turn to the place where I was born, to the mother who bore me and the father who taught me, long ago, long ago, long ago." See Alex's "Home, home, home, it was home I was wanting" and his actual return to "Home", Mr. Alexander's house in *Clockwork Orange*.

[9] V. Bérard, *Dans le sillage d'Ulysse*

[10] G. Poulet, *Les métamorphoses du cercle*, p 422

[11] L'Odyssée de Kubrick, in *Kubrick*, by Michel Ciment, p 33

[12] one may even talk of a chessboard technique.

[13] J. P. Dupuy, En mal du père, *Positif*, p 59

[14] G. Deleuze continues: "Regnault studied it concerning Hitchcock - as a result, in *Vertigo*, the big spiral can turn into the hero's fear of heights, as well as the circle he traces with his car or the curl in the heroin's hair." *L'image-mouvement*, p36

[15] S. Bernardi, *Le Regard esthétique ou la visibilité selon Kubrick*

[16] A. C. Clarke co-wrote the screenplay of *2001*. He is a renowned science-fiction novelist.

[17] P. Giuliani, *Stanley Kubrick*, p 90

[18] Thomas Allen Nelson writes about Barry Lyndon: "The temporal fabric of *Barry Lyndon* is made up of not only marriages and deaths but births and birthdays, old families and new families, first loves and last loves, friendships and sibling rivalries, quarrels and duels, games and debts: in other words, an elaborately ritualized parable of journeys begun and journeys ended." Kubrick, *Inside a Film Artist's Maze*, p 172

[19] J.P. Dupuy writes: "For lack of being able to raise and ennoble his name by linking it to the name of a very good stock, Barry Lyndon gives of himself in counterpart

of the debt that related him to the ghost of his wronged father. Our hero may be said to have punished himself for his Odyssey in the other world of aristocracy by exposing himself to the fury of whoever acts as his double: Bullingdon. By returning to Ireland, Barry returns to his mother who will now take care of him as when he was a child. At the end of the film then, both Barry and Bullingdon return to their respective mother, thus revealing their symmetry." En mal du père, *Positif*, p 61

[20] P. Giuliani, *Stanley Kubrick*, p 42-43

[21] Freddy Buache writes: "a citizen perfectly conditioned for the respect of official moral, Alex is presented a robotized bootlicker. Returned to social life, he is a prey for the revenge of his ancient acolytes and all those he tortured, but, at the same time, he is coddled by politicians who see in him - as he replaced rebellion by resignation - the model elector and the totally domesticated citizen." *Autour de Kubrick et Losey*, p 309

[22] A. Burgess, *A Clockwork Orange*, British Edition, p 195

[23] S. Kubrick, *A Clockwork Orange*, the screenplay, p 97-107

[24] The combat against the Cyclops is recurrent in Kubrick, a striking example is Davy's axe fight against Vinnie Rapallo in a cave-like warehouse filled with dislocated dummies.

[25] The *Übermensch* concept already appears in *Dr. Strangelove*, in its misunderstood version of the superior race which the Nazi magician Strangelove evokes, as well

as his wish to recreate the atmosphere of the old *Lebensborn* and its eugenic methods: a return to the caves, which antagonizes Zarathustra's.

[26] M. Ciment, *Kubrick*, p 130

[27] F. Nietzsche, *Thus spoke Zarathustra*, The Prologue, section three

[28] Kubrick declared: "Man must strive to gain mastery over himself as well as over his machines. Somebody has said that man is the missing link between primitive apes and civilized human beings. You might say that that idea is inherent in *2001*. We are semi-civilized, capable of cooperation and affection, but needing some sort of transfiguration into a higher form of life. Since the means to obliterate life on Earth exists, it will take more than just careful planning and reasonable cooperation to avoid some eventual catastrophe. The problem exists, and the problem is essentially a moral and spiritual one." Phillips, the Playboy interview in T.A. Nelson, p 100

[29] A detail of importance: HAL 9000 was to be called Athena, but Kubrick opted for a less apparent name.

[30] F. Nietzsche, *Ainsi parlait Zarathoustra*, Des trois métamorphoses

[31] See the animal references are battalions in Kubrick, in *Clockwork Orange*, for instance, Alex and the other prisoners sing a revealing hymn: "I was a wandering sheep, I was a wayward child, I did not love my home, I did not love my shepherd's voice, I would not be controlled," in

Spartacus, the slave-like gladiators are branded like animals.

[32] "A Journey beyond the Stars" was the shooting title of *2001* until Kubrick opted for a more Homeric title.

[33] Odysseus was a famous archer, the archery contest opposing Penelope's suitors is the twenty-first canto of Homer's Odyssey, the winner will marry Penelope. Disguised for his own safety, Odysseus is the only one able to string the bow, and therefore regains his wife and title. Eventually, he eliminates all the suitors with the same weapon.

[34] F. Nietzsche, *Ainsi parlait Zarathoustra*, Des vieilles et des nouvelles tables, section 1 to 3.

[35] G. Deleuze, *L'image-temps*, p 268-269

[36] M. Ciment, *Kubrick*, p 130

[37] In 1968, *2001* was received with antagonist feelings. It was a must for all LSD adepts.

[38] Harward Crimson: the floor and the food are specifically within Bowman's immediate frame of reference

[39] S. Kauffmann, Lost in the Stars: "Imagine zooming millions of miles - all those tiresome enclosed days, even weeks - to live inside a space suit. Kubrick makes the paradox graphic. Space only seems large. For human beings, it is confining. That is why, despite the size of the starry firmament, the idea of space travel gives me claustrophobia." The room aroused various reactions indeed. Kubrick calls it "a hospital room: a human zoo

approximating a hospital terrestrial environment drawn out of his dreams and imagination."

[40] Annette Michelson

[41] Harvey Greenberg

[42] God is a sphere the center of which is everywhere, the circumference nowhere.

[43] S. Kubrick, *Playboy* interview

[44] F. Nietzsche, *Ainsi parlait Zarathoustra*, The Prologue, section two

[45] Stanley Kubrick in Eric Norden, Interview with Stanley Kubrick, *Playboy*, Sept. 1968, in Nelson, p 17

[46] T. A. Nelson writes: "*Fear and Desire* begins with a Conrad-sounding poem in voiceover, continues with an array of subjective devices as we watch four soldiers wander through an imaginary forest, and concludes with a penetration out of a collective heart of darkness into a dawn of new understanding. Lieutenant Corby (Kenneth Harp), the intellectual, discovers the fictitious nature of rationalism as he symbolically kills himself by killing his double, a Nazi general officer (also played by Kenneth Harp), while Mac (Frank Silvera), the primitive, fights through his rage and paranoia in a misty raft trip downriver. The themes of the film are out of a grab-bag of 1950s bohemian negativism (the film attacks war and other social institutions and it shows the failures of reason and the dangers of an unexplored unconscious) and existential self-congratulation. (When James Mason as Humbert in

Lolita pretends to be going to Hollywood to make a film about existentialism, which, he ironically tells us, was a "hot thing" at the time, Kubrick may be telling us something about his early work.) T. A. Nelson, *Stanley Kubrick*, p 21

[47] B. Pascal, *Pensées et Opuscules*, Brunschvicg Edition, p 646

[48] Relating the anguish of man to his evolution Freddy Buache writes that: "From the egg in which the opalescent fetus is curled up to the Milky Way of Milky Ways, man asserts himself, grows, dies and is reborn, free to build up his destiny, mastering nature always more, repulsing anguish by action, falling back from his grand victories to the original anguish and - always richer in science and enlightenment - incessantly disappearing in the night of Non-Science... To express these double truths of the Nietzschean meditation - Man, Superman, Gay Science, Non-Science - joined together by the myth of Eternal Return, Kubrick relied entirely on the specificity of the cinematographic language. He banished explanatory dialogues, plots, dramatic tensions and narrative logics essentially to take advantage of the visual rhythms' orchestration. From the science-fiction novel he moves on to the moral tale, then he cuts the ultimate moorings of rationality, smashes the Old Tables and hurls the poem in full lyrical abstraction to conduct it on the other side of the mirror." *Le cinéma anglais autour de Kubrick et Losey*, p 303-307

[49] G. Poulet, *Les métamorphoses du cercle*

[50] Michel Sineux writes, anguish is also felt in the musical selection, as in *The Shining*: "The descending third of Berlioz's allegretto, which gives rhythm to *The Shining*'s dolly movements of the credits, prefigures the irrevocability of Jack's mental voyage. The other musical selections are contemporary borrowings - Bartok, Ligeti, Penderecki - which experiment each in its own way through language researches the disarray of contemporary man in front of his maladjustment with the world and the failure of his beliefs, as well as the resulting splitting of his personality." La symphonie Kubrick, *Positif*, p 36

[51] M. Ciment, *Kubrick*, p 122 Ciment quotes Wiener: "As Norbert Wiener says: we are shipwreck victims on a planet destined to die." Pessimistic too is A.C. Clarke's conception: "Behind everyman now alive stand thirty ghosts, for that is the ratio by which the dead outnumber the living. Since the dawn of time, roughly a hundred billion human beings have walked the planet earth. Now this is an interesting number, for by a curious coincidence there are approximately a hundred billion stars in our local universe, the Milky Way. So, for every man who has ever lived in the universe, there shines a star. But every one of these stars is a sun often far more brilliant and glorious than the small, nearby star we call the sun. And many perhaps most, of those alien suns have planets circling them. So almost certainly there is enough land in the sky

to give every member of the human species, back to the first ape-man, his own private world-sized heaven or hell." A.C. Clarke, *2001*. Foreword.

[52] A. Koyré, *Du monde clos à l'univers infini*, p 10

[53] The towels in the bathroom and the cutlery on the table are meticulously, symmetrically positioned.

[54] A Promethean equation can be found between Zarathustra and Dr. Strangelove: "If I ever - at the table of gods which is the earth - played dice with the gods so that the earth would tremble, break and spit rivers of fire: for the earth is a table for the gods, which trembles under the new, creative words, and when the gods throw their dice." F. Nietzsche, *Ainsi parlait Zarathoustra*, The Seven Seals, section three

The war room of *Dr. Strangelove* cannot be describe with more aptness, for as Ken Adam, *Dr. Strangelove*'s designer, said: "When I thought about this big circular table, Stanley told me: 'this is interesting because it looks like a gigantic Poker table. And this president, these generals play with the world as with cards." M. Ciment, Entretien avec Ken Adam, De James Bond à Barry Lyndon, *Positif*, p 29. In a way, this also refers to the game tables of Barry Lyndon, which allow Barry to reach the high spheres of nobility.

[55] P. Sellier, Le mythe du héros ou le désir d'être dieu, p 14-15

[56] "The hero is always imagined with traits borrowed from the Sun. The Sun itself follows its course, of which the different stages are easily assimilated to a brilliant life.

Unlike the Moon, which is imagined as dead, during the moment of obscurity, the sun seems to have gone down in the kingdom of darkness, in the underworld, which he crosses without being touched by death." Le mythe du héros ou le désir d'être Dieu, p 18-19

[57] "The Dawn of Man" is the title of the first episode of *2001*'s quadrilogy. Paradoxically, the second episode of the film – Dr. Floyd's going to the lunar base - is continuous to "The Dawn of Man", the fusion being total between the Pleistocene era and the third millenary. "Jupiter Mission, 18 months later" is third, this is Bowman's apparition; "Jupiter and Beyond the Infinite" is fourth.

[58] Alex's course is ascending in brutality, stagnating in prison, descending in brutality with the treatment, to be ascending again in his rebirth-like suicide. Barry's is ascending in the first part and descending in the second to be ascending again if one follows William Thackeray's *Barry Lyndon*, from which the film originates. Jack's may also be included: descending in rationality and ascending in madness to be descending again in the darkness of the Overlook Hotel.

[59] "ces regards fulgurants qui, semblables à ceux de Napoléon, brisaient les volontés et les cerveaux." Balzac in Sellier, p 19. The flame-throwing eyes of Napoleon. Napoleon is Kubrick's lifelong, unaccomplished project.

[60] The Eternal Return of the Being, as Karl Löwith writes is: "The eternally returning cycle of he who is born

and disappears, in which the Being's perennity and the changes of becomingness are one and only... The voyage of the new Columbus towards the dusk of the Being on the borders of nothingness to be born again on the borders of the Being." Nietzsche et la philosophie de l'éternel retour du même, p 10 Or as Jean Granier:.".. a constant and infinite force, spreading in a finite space in accordance with a becomingness into which everything repeats itself, a perpetual cycle..." *Nietzsche*, p 107-110

[61] The centrifugal Odysseus

[62] G. Poulet, *Les métamorphoses du cercle*, p 159

[63] P. Valéry, *Degas Danse Dessin*, p 1172

[64] Michel Ciment writes: "the last shot of *The Shining* introduces a new development, which opens the story, an opening on another time and another space -reincarnation; arrival or return of a new lodger-ghost."

[65] F. Nietzsche, *Ainsi parlait Zarathoustra*, le convalescent, section 2

[66] Otto Weininger, Des fins ultimes, in K. Löwith, Nietzsche et la philosophie de l'éternel retour du même, p199-200

[67] Kubrick once remarked that the Von Karajan version of *The Blue Danube* is ideal for depicting grace and beauty in turning. It also gets about as far away as you can get from the cliché of space music (Agel Jerome, the making of *2001*, 1970)

[68] See Burgess's belief that human beings and societies are part of a cyclical process moving back and forth in time

between goodness and evil, totalitarianism and freedom. This also refers to HAL as the superior mechanism controlling the lives of the astronauts, and the science-fictional theme of the machines' control of man which is found in the Doomsday machine of *Dr. Strangelove*. Finally, this refers to the military machine of *Full Metal Jacket*.

[69] The twin sisters to Danny: "Hello, Danny, come and play with us for ever and ever and ever."

Jack to Danny: "I wish we could stay here for ever and ever and ever."

Grady to Jack: "You've always been the caretaker. I should know, I've always been here."

[70] P. Giuliani, *Stanley Kubrick*, p 42-43

[71] J.L. Bourget, Les avatars du cercle, *Positif* n° 136, March 1972

[72] Thierry Cazals writes: "asexual, sterilized, spatial version of North by North-West, *2001* is a vertiginous Odyssey of our fleeing forward, on board of vehicles (here, spaceships) or under missions in trompe l'oeil, finishing with the hope of a rebirth beyond the apparent death, the "diving in the tunnel" L'homme-Labyrinthe, *Cahiers du cinéma*, p 24

[73] T.A. Nelson, *Kubrick, Inside a film artist's maze*, p 120
S. Bernardi writes: "the capital breakthrough of the spaceship Discovery indicates the beginning of a reverse movement towards the past. The analogy here suggested

between macrocosm and microcosm, between the nebula and the living cell, suggests the theme of impregnation." *Le regard esthétique ou la visibilité selon Kubrick*, p 153

[74] M. Ciment, *Kubrick*, p 134

[75] T. A. Nelson writes: "Jack's passion for the enclosed order of the maze resembles the Navajo circle that protects one from malevolent outside forces, except that Kubrick's films usually reverse that mythology and characterize such world as entrapping, while outside space offers both uncertain exploration and hope. Like the maze, however, the Indian circle has an opening (the East) for both entrance and escape. Throughout the film, Danny is associated with circles. These, although they recall the Navajo circle of protection from outside evil, ironically enclose rather than banish the evil that exists inside his home (the circle/maze of Jack's madness)."T. A. Nelson, Kubrick, *Inside a Film Artist's Maze*, p 262. For a discussion of Navajo sand paintings, their mythology and symbolism see Leland Wyman, *The Windways of the Navaho*.

[76] "Danny moves in a circle around the Colorado Lounge on his Big Wheels tricycle, while Jack tends to remain stationary within its center, Wendy and Danny explore the hedge maze and complete a circular course from inside space back into outside space." T.A. Nelson, Kubrick, *Inside a film artist's maze*, p 207

[77] Grady would be Teiresias, the caretaker of Hades

[78] For poltergeists they must be, especially when they knock on the door of Jack's jail-like food shed

[79] L. Hautecoeur, *Symbolisme du cercle et de la coupole*, p 40

[80] About the magic circles of *Dr Strangelove*, Jean Philippe Domecq writes: "The double or triple circles - abstract and magic - which the authorities surround with in Dr. Strangelove and which separate the decisive light from the scheming's obscurity until the fraction line between strategy and frenzy breaks." *Un voyage dans l'espace de Kubrick*, p 46

[81] See the chess-game symbolism: the combat of Darkness against Light, Titans against Gods, the stakes being the supremacy on the world

[82] T. A. Nelson noted: "on one side we have the battle-line represented by the five judges symmetrically composed with the Colonel Judge in the middle, framed by an archway in the background and the French flag overhead; on the other, the three prisoners, sitting in chairs, enclosed from behind like pawns by two lines of guards standing motionless in an attitude of parade rest." Kubrick, Inside a Film Artist's Maze, p 48

[83] T.A. Nelson, Kubrick, *Inside a film artist's maze*, p 77

[84] Charlotte to Humbert: "You're going to take my Queen", at the same time Lolita kisses Humbert goodbye.

[85] P. Giuliani, *Stanley Kubrick*, p 42

[86] *The Shining* may be seen as a parody of *The Return of the Living Dead*, or another famous return: *The Return of Dracula*.

[87] M. Ciment, *Kubrick*, p 146. Paolo Santarcangeli, *Le livre des labyrinthes*, Gallimard, Paris, 1974, 430p

[88] F. Buache, *Le cinéma anglais autour de Kubrick et Losey*, p 303-307

[89] G. Poulet, *Les métamorphoses du cercle*, p 75

[90] Sandro Bernardi writes: "Hogarth quotes Lomazzo: it is said that Michelangelo said once to Da Siena, his student, that he always had to draw a pyramidal, serpentine figure, multiplied once, twice and thrice. In the wake of Lomazzo, Hogarth rediscovered this torsion and theorized it in his treaty. Sterne derided it with much witticism; Kubrick re-used it not only in 2001, but in most of his portraits." *Le regard esthétique ou la visibilité selon Kubrick.* p 157

[91] Including Gainsborough, Fragonard, Constable, Stubbs, and Reynold.

[92] D. Bindman, Hogarth, p 154-155

[93] T. Gray (1716-1771), *An Elegy written in a Country Churchyard*, 1751

[94] T. A. Nelson, Kubrick, *Inside a Film Artist's Maze*, p 43

[95] It also recalls Humbert's entrance in Quilty's house, as he walks through the room, passes round a harp and finishes his sinuous course at the Ping-Pong table.

[96] S. Bernardi, *Le regard esthétique ou la visibilité selon Kubrick*, p 56

[97] G. Poulet, *Les métamorphoses du cercle*, p 75

[98] Ibid. p 76-78

[99] Davy's first words, in the train station: "it's crazy how you can get yourself in a mess sometimes."

[100] See A. Koyré, *Du monde clos à l'univers infini*

[101] In A.C. Clarke's version, the monolith not only manipulates the subconscious of the pre-historic hominids but also their gestures and reflexes. Clarke's monolith is transparent and reflects the sun light.

[102] T. Cazals writes: "The monolith remains to this day the only example of a beneficial superior being, of a successful projection. For it is not a screen of harmonization, of standardization - Hollywood - but a passing through screen, a door presaging a Beyond of the Show and of humanity. The monolith does not function as a screen for projection, on which we could revive our psychoses through transference, but as a place of perdition. We must lose sight of ourselves and dissolve in the schizophrenic seeing - Bowman's chain splitting - before the ultimate remodeling of our humanity. 2001 is something like a deprogrammed clone of cinema seeking to deify itself." *L'homme-Labyrinthe*, Cahiers du cinéma, p 26

[103] *Playboy* interview with Kubrick.

[104] Alex says: "it's funny how colors of the real world seems really real when you viddy them on a screen", Screenplay, p 59. Corroboratively, the FAQ writes: "Because the apparatus presents not a world to explore, but a screen upon which images are projected, Alex, like a

prisoner in Plato's cave, is afflicted, willingly/unwillingly, with a type of motor paralysis which makes the reality test impractical him. He is reduced to a subject remotely controlled by the cinematic apparatus and science. That this is perceived pleasurably for the mass audience might be linked to a regression to a state of infant-like passivity. As passive subjects, the camera's eye becomes our eye, and its distortions become, possibly, the truth. It is not his mind but his body which learns this connection. Here, that chosen passivity is revealed to be what it denies, Alex like us, is a willing victim."

[105] Kubrick declared: "I like the slow start, the start that goes under the audience's skin and involves them so that they can appreciate grace notes and soft tones and don't have to be pounded over the head with plot points and suspense hooks." in Nelson, *Inside a Film Artist's Maze*, p 10

[106] Dudley Andrew, André Bazin (New York: Oxford U P, 1978, p 121)

[107] T. Cazals, L'homme-Labyrinthe, *Cahiers du cinéma*, p 23

[108] S. Bernardi writes: "The obstinate search for contradiction is constant in Kubrick and we find it everywhere to create paralogisms and antinomies, to oppose the filmic language with the story told, to set pictures against signification, to authenticate what clearly appeared as false from the start - the amphibologies of the cinematographic picture." *Le regard esthétique ou la visibilité selon Kubrick*, p37

[109] about the symbol of God, Freddy Buache writes: this symbol is not one, it is the crystallization of all symbols, the fulcrum of creative conscience and the limit, tracing the finishing line of our most extraordinary intellectual adventures, and the starting line beyond which everything - in spite of all that have been accomplished regarding action - is still to be accomplished... It will always - until the end of time - fascinate men in quest of infinity but condemned to finitude, though they carry infinity with them as their life - by the power of dream - is a flame stolen from the fire of eternity. Indeed, the dream disintegrates on the threshold of death which, like the monolith, is both an end and a beginning. The solitary explorer launched till the end of life, to the deepest and farthest abyss of time and space, must admit that he has only covered a ridiculous distance, a few million miles, when, ahead of him, stand billions of billions of light years to cross. He has grown old, doubled and thinks he has stridden over a good bit of territory. How illusory!" Le cinéma anglais autour de Kubrick et Losey, p 303-307

[110] See A.C. Clarke, *The Sentinel*

[111] G. Deleuze: "The black stone of 2001 presides over both cosmic and cerebral states: it is the soul of the three bodies: Earth, Moon, Sun but also the seed of the three brains: animal, human, mechanical." *L'image-temps*, p 268-269

[112] See William Blake: "If the doors of perception were

cleansed, everything would appear to man as it is, infinite." Confucius: "The way out is through the door."

[113] S. Bernardi, *Le regard esthétique ou la vision selon Kubrick*, p 119 Bernardi produces a series of interpretations, among which are Benayoun's and Sontag's: "Kubrick's style produces uninterpretable movies and puts the reading to the test like the research of a hidden signification to be discovered. The critic finds himself in front of a deadlock, a kind of Rorschach test, in which anything may be said indifferently - each one finds himself, in fear or delight."(R. Benayoun)"The film is an unassailable monolith, its interpretation is in fact the model Kubrick eludes constantly. Interpreting signifies impoverishing."(S. Sontag) p 38 About *2001*'s compression, Nelson writes: "*2001* compresses the action of the novel, omitting expository scenes and narration, and creating, in effect, a series of ellipses. The audience must fill the gaps through a combination of visual attentiveness and subliminal penetration, an associative rather than strictly visual structure." *Inside a Film Artist's Maze*, p 103. Describing the absence of meaning as a dangerous exaltation of the vision, Bernardi writes: "Like silence which exalts the power of speech according to Diderot, seeing that we do not see exalts the power of vision. The spectator can also surpass the experience of the Baudelairian stroller, who walks until he sees the invisible, risking - as in a film by Corman - to tear his eyes out." p 24

[114] F. Ferrini writes in *Bianco e Nero*, n°10, that the

monolith is a dissolve to dark, that is to say, cinema itself in the making. Given by Bernardi, p 119

[115] S. Bernardi, *Le regard esthétique ou la vision selon Kubrick*, p 102 Again Bernardi writes: "the film speaks about the spectator to the spectators." He also quotes B. Balàzs: "between this seeing and this seeing that we do not see the interminable game between sense and signification is played. "Der Sichtbare Mensch, D.O.V, Wien-Leipzig, 1924 in Bernardi, p 161. This enhances the mirror effect of the monolith, we come to see ourselves seeing.

[116] This is why Bernardi feels the need to establish a differentiation between the strong spectator and the weak: "insidiously, the film attracts us inside ourselves with the only purpose of making us lose our own traces. Cinema looks for a strong spectator, capable of running the risk inherent to any abnormal visual experience, capable of using and abusing the film itself, of moving in a pluri-centric universe –the complete opposite of the weak spectator, usually presupposed by classic narrative cinema which prescribes and demands a normative behavior. Contemporary cinema adventures on the territories of the possible, opening perception, opening the windows of the sense." p 159 What is more interesting in Bernardi's differentiation - as regards our Odysseus-like spectator - is the image of "the strong spectator which presents himself in front of the work, equipped with his indispensable instruments of study: a system of expectancy and

interpretative codes - but he is ready to put everything at stake again without modifying his instruments, even lose them or, as De Man says, confront blindness so as to find vision again..." *Le regard esthétique ou la visibilité selon Kubrick*, p 106

[117] T.A. Nelson, Kubrick, *Inside a Film Artist's Maze*, p 229

[118] Pierre Giuliani writes: "Kubrick's cinema invents new forms and invites us to break with them. From going in the clarity of its methods to destroying them, Kubrick's cinema also preserves, morally, a tendency to self-immolation. " *Stanley Kubrick*, p 23

[119] T. Cazals, *L'homme-labyrinthe*, p 24   Concurrently, Nelson writes: "how does a film maker give form to something "beyond the infinite" without a loss of thematic integrity or narrative clarity? For a start, he can undermine the authority of objective temporal structures - that is, the continuities of plot, character, dialogue, narration - and require an audience to scan his images and sounds for an associative or symbolic logic." *Inside a Film Artist's Maze*, p129. Sandro Bernardi writes: "a constellation of meanings, an eclipse of the signifying function and an opening on the visible, the experience of the filmic vision is a kind of voyage which starts from the conceptual schemas of the film as well as of the discourse, and moves away from them only to return better still." S. Bernardi, *Le regard esthétique ou la visibilité selon Kubrick*, p 17. An Odyssean circularity is to be found in Kubrick's dialectics,

it is clear.

[120] S. Bernardi speaks of a path: "The cinema which brings the eye's contradictions to light, like Kubrick's does, constrains us to take a difficult path which dismantles the models and forms of representation, and induces us to confront objects very distant from one another and construct, if necessary, a different theory for each object." *Le regard esthétique ou la visibilité selon Kubrick*, p 21

[121] See Fredric Jameson's chapter on *The Shining*'s historicism in his *Signatures of the Visible*, p 82-98

[122] Molina-Foix, Entretien avec Stanley Kubrick, *Cahiers du cinéma*, p 7

[123] On Freud's approach to strangeness, Bernardi writes: "the unknown is hidden within the known: one has only to change eyes, change looks or objective to discover in the familiar or the domestic an insoluble strangeness, an infinite complexity without destiny nor signification." Le regard esthétique ou la visibilité selon Kubrick, p 35. What is so strange about *The Shining* is that it stands at the frontier of the possible, between what we tolerate as reality and as fiction. *The Shining* is a gigantic doubt.

[124] Nelson writes: "For Kubrick, the aesthetics of his medium likewise are tools of expression, mythopoeic extensions for the inner complexities of his vision, an opportunity for converting cinematic form into cinematic meanings." *Inside a Film Artist's Maze*, p 19

[125] See Michael Henry & Michel Ciment & Michel

Cieutat, Positif n°320, Oct. 1987

[126] Anecdotally, *Full Metal Jacket* is a film about war and Vietnam with very few war scenes which are entirely shot in the London suburbia.

[127] S. Bernardi writes: "The building is a substitution more than an analogy with which an infinite number of association is possible: an allusion to the Bauhaus, a symbol of communism, Hitler's fortifications, despotism, first level of ambiguity, of *coincidentia oppositorum*." le regard esthétique ou la visibilité selon Kubrick, p 34

[128] P. Giuliani, *Stanley Kubrick*, p 188

[129] T. A. Nelson writes that: "*Clockwork Orange* becomes a trompe l'oeil, Kubrick's reflection on his cinematic past, one that puts an audience, like Bowman, in a strange room and demands it look for signs of an unseen intelligence." *Inside a Film Artist's Maze*, p 144

[130] M. Ciment, *Kubrick*, p 81

[131] Kubrick also admitted other borrowings from his masters, Sergei Eisenstein, Charlie Chaplin, Ophüls. He declared that: "anyone seriously interested in the differences between cinematographic techniques should study Eisenstein and Chaplin. With Eisenstein all is form and no content whereas with Chaplin all is content and no form. in M. Ciment, *Kubrick*, p 34

[132] Kubrick declared: "I think that one of the biggest mistakes of 20th century Art is the obsession with originality at all costs. Great innovators like Beethoven did not cut off totally from the art that preceded them. To

innovate is to steam ahead without abandoning the past."

[133] T. Cazals writes: "Drifting like a satellite in the cinema-galaxy Kubrick's work gravitates around two founding Suns that are Lumière and Méliès. On the one hand, the passion for realism, the objective movement, and the birth of the mathematics of the forms in full light. On the other, the raging pressure of metamorphoses, the phantom of ubiquity, the emergence of an alchemy of the surfacing and the retractable... Kubrick's cinema is located at the crossroads, the meeting point of mechanism and the living, myth and abstraction, magical ecstasy and simulation. At the same time eccentric (vis-à-vis Hollywood's standards and studios) and "right in the center" (in search of the Gordian knots on which the duality and ambiguity of Man are read, Kubrick has substituted the Majors' know-how (systematically aiming at the average spectator) for a learned knowledge keeping an eye on the centers of gravity of the modern world, centers towards which the maximum of forces converge even if they are those of generalized massacre, waste, madness or a perverse reform of humanity." *L'homme-labyrinthe*, p 23 - 24

[134] S. Bernardi, *Le regard esthétique ou la visibilité selon Kubrick*, p 28

[135] Jakob Bodmer, the father of modern criticism, wrote that: "the poet creates a whole within which the parts stand. Each work of art must therefore have a center."

Bernardi comments that: "if the work of art has a center around which the other parts are arranged to form a whole, it becomes possible to analyze the relations between the center and the parts and produce a new synthesis. The work of art is an organic whole which must be understood as such." *Le regard esthétique ou la visibilité selon Kubrick*, p 84

[136] T.A. Nelson, *Inside a Film Artist's Cave*, p 106 Following the macrocosmic example of Kubrick's lifework, Barry Lyndon is composed of a myriad of pictures: " In Barry Lyndon each composition is like a painting by one of the Old Masters, and they link one onto the other like the tiles of a wondrous mosaic (citing John Alcott, Director of Photography, The American Cinematographer essay, p270)", p 261

[137] Humbert: "Are you Quilty?" Quilty: "No, I'm Spartacus; have you come to free the slaves or something?"

[138] S. Kubrick, *A Clockwork Orange*, the script, p 3

[139] A solar characteristic discussed earlier

[140] José Gil's *homo americanus bellicosus*, their ruthlessness recalling their simian ancestors'

[141] M. Ciment noted that the similitude between both films appears in their very titles: *Full Metal Jacket / Clockwork Orange*, a mixing of mechanical and living. Comparing the Kubrickian parallelisms, Henry Michael utilizes a circular explanation: "First circle from hell: Parris Island evokes both the penitentiary universe and the mental hospital or, in other words, the stooges of *Dr Strangelove* and the punks of *Clockwork Orange*. Second

circle from hell: a battlefield, a chaotic zone with vague contours, shook by periodic explosions." "Paint it Black", à propos de *Full Metal Jacket*. *Positif*, p 42. Kubrick's films could be seen as circles within circles, extending therefore the Odyssean circularity. On this subject, P. Giuliani writes: "*2001* is a film of ascension and *The Shining* of fall; they both exchange a great number of irreversible pictures. They both mark the two extremities of an arc of a circle that we must imagine as tending towards the perfect circle, as if their reason of being was to become circular." *Stanley Kubrick*, p 78.

[142] Michel Ciment writes: "The film maker has always been concerned with historical fractures, whether they be the premises for the collapse of the antique world, the nuclear catastrophe, world war one, or the imminent crisis of the Age of Enlightenment, Kubrick is fascinated by these periods in which the world is overbalanced, this turning point being the objective correlative of the individuals' loss of control of their destiny." *Kubrick*, p 238

[143] Robert Benayoun: "It is as if Kubrick had decided to settle in the famous white room where past meets future" *Le Point*. Jan. 5th, 1976

[144] Sando Bernardi writes: "The artistic creation has a cathartic function indeed, like the myth as Kubrick seems to tell us, as he has always wanted to link his films to the collective imagination. The film maker creates for the greatest number archetypal works of art, carriers of myths

in which the spectators will find an appeasement to their torments and desires." *Le regard esthétique ou la visibilité selon Kubrick*, p 34

[145] Nelson writes: "Films today present us with a totally contingent universe, where images and sounds mean both nothing and everything, a world of total probability and zero signification. And this cinema of contingency finds no fuller expression than in the films of Stanley Kubrick... An awareness of contingency arises whenever there is a loss of faith in teleological explanations, in the received or discovered validity of meaning, in the rational structures of nature or the signifying power of mind and language. His films, from the efforts of Johnny Clay to control the exigencies of time and space in *The Killing* to *Barry Lyndon*'s entrapment within the psychological and historical forms of his ambition or Jack's journey in *The Shining* through the mazes of a collective unconscious, repeatedly investigate the human and aesthetic consequences of contingency." *Inside a Film Artist's Cave*, p 1-19

[146] P. Giuliani, *Stanley Kubrick*, p 66

[147] T.A. Nelson writes: "Kubrick's wit is especially evident when he shows Davy struggling with the telephone cord in his eagerness to see Gloria directly through the window; his frustration is matched by the audience's, as its attention wavers between Davy on screen right talking on the phone and Gloria undressing in mirror reflection on screen left. The apartment light goes off, the mirror image turns to black, and the camera holds on Davy, standing

and waiting as if he expected that dream in the mirror to magically reappear." *Inside a Film Artist's Cave*, p 26

[148] Cocteau said: "Les miroirs feraient bien de réfléchir un peu avant de renvoyer les images" in Giuliani, p 77

[149] See Fritz Lang's use of mirror effects and reflections as revealing of true nature and monstrosity

[150] Nelson writes: "Alex is later the victim of a savage retribution at the hands of his civilized double (Mr Alexander), long before Alex becomes the Frankenstein monster of a clockwork state, social communication has degenerated into an impersonal and sterile intercourse - masculine with masculine, feminine with feminine, objects with objects. Alex disturbs this reflexive séance - and becomes the only regenerative force in the film - because he embodies the concept of the Other, society's nemesis rather than child, more doppelgänger than twin." *Inside a Film Artist's Cave*, p 146

[151] T.A. Nelson, Inside a Film Artist's Cave, p 155

[152] "Les coeurs l'un par l'autre attirés/ Se communiquent leur substance/ Tels deux miroirs ardents/ Concentrent la lumière et se la réfléchissent/ Les rayons tour à tour recueillis ... divisés/ En se multipliant / S'accroissent, s'embellissent/Et d'autant plus actifs/ Qu'ils se sont plus croisés/ Au même point se réunissent." in Ciment p 110

[153] P. Giuliani writes: "The theme of the alter ego emphasizes the fact that Quilty is another Humbert.

Humbert's murderous act would be nothing else but a self-punishment, a self-effacement, which confirms Humbert's death some time later: one do not outlive one's double loss." Stanley Kubrick, p 50 Nelson writes: "Now, Quilty-like, Humbert will add incest to his sins and so begin a journey into a nightmare where Quilty's presence, alternately spectral and corporeal, will provide a mirror image for both his own sexual degradation and Lolita's triviality." *Inside a Film Artist's Maze*, p 67

[154] See M. Ciment, *Kubrick*, p 232

[155] Kubrick's first short movie in 1951, cf. Sandro Bernardi, p 132

[156] T. A. Nelson, Inside a Film Artist's Maze, p 100

[157] As Thierry Cazals writes: "Kubrick's cinema leads to absurdity the logic of dissolution which already governs the laceration of humanity, the divorce of the look and the bodies: to feel oneself a body, it is already knowing oneself an image, destined to fragmentation, to partiality, to the limit, as Christine Glucksmann writes in her essay on Baroque aestheticism, La folie du voir." *L'homme-labyrinthe*, p 25

[158] Michel Cieutat on the circular-cellular American family: "Circle figures are recurrent in American movies, they either represent the need for a maternal protection, or even the keeping of the family's unity. In western movies, when a caravan of covered wagons forms a circle against an Indian attack. It is around a circular table that Richard Thorpe's knights gather... it is in a crystal ball handled by

Orson Welles that Tuesday Weld, in *A Safe Place*, looks back in his childhood and his past which he cannot escape, it is the image of a circle with a triangle at its center which appears on the computer's screen during the fertilization of Julie Christie by Proteus IV in *Demon Seed*. From this mating a new race will rise, like the end of *2001*, when the encircled fetus, symbolizing the future of humanity, becomes the equal of the earth... The American family circle rejoins the circle of earthly paradise, of the alliance with the celestial God. The future of the elected people relies on the fact that the circle remains untouched., *Les grands thèmes du cinéma américain*, Tome 1: le rêve et le cauchemar, p56-7

[159] M. Ciment, Kubrick, p 98

[160] Nelson writes: "Burgess's ironic reflection on civilized pretenses, even to the point of diminishing the moral authority of its own linguistic instrument through Alex's Nadsat ("civilized my syphilized yarbles") recalls the devaluation of words and forms in *Paths of Glory*, *Lolita*, *Dr. Strangelove*, and *2001*." *Inside a Film Artist's Cave*, p 139

[161] Pierre Giuliani: "A dialogue is less an exchange and more a crossing of two heterogeneous speeches. The characters speak more to dissimulate their feelings and their goals than to express them. Language is a weapon, sometimes a duel - HAL-Bowman, sometimes a dialogue of the deaf." Stanley Kubrick

[162] For instance, "Mission Control, this is X-ray-Delta-

One. At two-zero-four-five, on-board fault prediction center in our nine-triple-zero computer showed Alpha Echo three five unit..." in Nelson, p 254

[163] B. Krohn, Le film-cerveau, *Full Metal Jacket*, *Cahiers du cinéma*, p10-11 M. Ciment writes: "The prologue on Parris Island forms a film per se - the cellular structure of the story evokes both 2001's, the apes sequence like the training camp's foretelling a long journey - is opposed to the Vietnam episodes, as order to disorder." Kubrick, p 234

[164] For instance, Pyle is defined as a "Section A" when his derangement becomes uncontrollable

[165] P. Giuliani writes:" The dialogues and songs of *Full Metal Jacket* are a mixture of death and sex, morbid sex, mortifying, mortified, and sexualized death, foreboding the general construction of the film like some kind of mortiferous orgasm. Stanley Kubrick, p 51

[166] T. Cazals, L'homme-labyrinthe, *Cahiers du cinéma*, p24. This paper came out a few years before *Eyes Wide Shut* and cites 12 films instead of 13.

[167] For instance, in *Lolita*: Mrs. Haze to Quilty: "my daughter is going to have a cavity filled by your uncle Ivor, the local dentist" which makes Quilty knowingly smirks. Or Jean Farlow, Mrs. Haze's friend, to Humbert: "you know Humbert, John and I are very broad-minded... extremely broad-minded."

[168] Nelson writes about Lolita: "Kubrick could not sufficiently dramatize the erotic aspect of Humbert's obsession with the nymphet." *Inside a Film Artist's Cave*,

p 63

[169] Nelson writes: "the sexual content of Dr. Strangelove, what Anthony Macklin labels a "sex allegory" and George Linden calls an example of "erotic displacement", represents the most discernible and widely discussed mythopoeic element in the film." *Inside a Film Artist's Cave*, p 89

[170] In Nelson: "a reference to vulva, and even though both "merkin" and "muffley" suggest a covering, he is bald, which makes his head look like a phallus." p 91

[171] Alex: "we were all feeling a bit shagged and fagged and fashed, it having been an evening of some small energy expenditure, O my Brothers... " *A Clockwork Orange,* the screenplay, p 10. Alex: "there were naked devotchkas ripped and creeching against walls and I plunging like a shlaga into them." p 15

[172] Sex is so explicit in *Eyes Wide Shut* that it turned into a battle between censored vs uncensored. In order to avoid the uneconomical NC-17 Rating – no one 17 and under is admitted in theatres – in the United States, Warner Bros. first released a cut version of the movie to theatres where most of the orgy scenes were covered by computer generated persons standing in the foreground. Consequently, the movie received the R-Rating whereas the worldwide releases were all based on the original unedited version. The unrated version was later released on DVD and Blu-ray in the United States.

Bibliography

Abrams, Jerold (2007). *The Philosophy of Stanley Kubrick*. University Press of Kentucky.

Agel, Jérôme (1970). *The Making of Kubrick's 2001*. New American Library.

Althaus, Benjamin (2004). *Communication in Stanley Kubrick's "Eyes Wide Shut."* Grin Verlag.

Appel, Alfred (1974). *Nabokov's Dark Cinema*. New York, Oxford University Press,

Bane, Charles (2006). *Viewing Novels, Reading Films: Stanley Kubrick and the Art of Adaptation as Interpretation*. Louisiana State University and Agricultural & Mechanical College.

Barbier, Denis (1981) Entretien avec Diane Johnson (Shining). *Positif*, January 1981, n° 238, p20-25

Baxter, John (1998). *Stanley Kubrick: A Biography*. HarperCollins Publishers Limited.

Benson, Michael (2018). *Space Odyssey: Stanley Kubrick, Arthur C. Clarke, and the Making of a Masterpiece*. Simon and Schuster.

Berard, Victor (1924). *Dans le sillage d'Ulysse*. Paris.

Bernardi, Sandro (1994). *Le regard esthétique ou la visibilité selon Kubrick.* Translated from Italian by Laure Raffaeli-Fournier, Saint-Denis, Presse Universitaire de Vincennes.

Bindman, David (1981). *Hogarth*, New York, Thames and Hudson.

Böttcher, Heiko (2007). *The Metamorphosis of Alex in Stanley Kubrick's 'Clockwork Orange' from a Viewpoint of Abnormal Psychology.* Grin Verlag.

Bourget, Jean-Loup (1985). *Le cinéma américain, 1895-1980.* Presse Universitaire de France

Brion, Patrick. (1994) *Le cinéma fantastique, du monde perdu à 2001.* Editions de Martinière.

Brown, Garret (1981). Shining et la steadycam. *Positif*, February 1981, n° 239, p37-44

Buache. Freddy (1978). *Autour de Kubrick et Losey.* Lausanne, éditions l'âge d'or.

Buache, Freddy (1974). *Le cinéma américain, 1955-1970.* Editions l'âge d'homme.

Burgess, Anthony (1962). *L'orange mécanique.* Translated from English by Georges Belmont & Hortense Chabrier, Paris, Robert Laffont.

Burgess, Anthony (2000). *Stanley Kubrick's a Clockwork Orange*: Based on the Novel by Anthony Burgess. Screen Press Books.

Castle, Alison (2005). *The Stanley Kubrick Archives.* Taschen.

Cazals, Thierry (1980). L'homme-Labyrinthe. *Cahiers du cinéma*, November 1980, n° 317, p23-29

Chion, Michel (2001). *Kubrick's cinema odyssey*. British Film Institute.

Cieutat, Michel (1987). Hollywood et le Viêt-nam. *Positif*, October 1987, n° 320, p50-58

Cieutat, Michel (1988). *Les grands thèmes du cinéma américain. Tome 1 : le rêve et le cauchemar*, Paris, Les Editions du Cerf.

Ciment, Michel (1977). Entretien avec Ken Adam, De James Bond à Barry Lyndon. *Positif*, March 1977, p26-39

Ciment, Michel (1987). Entretien avec Michael Herr, scénariste. *Positif*, October 1987, n° 320, p43-49

Ciment, Michel (1988). *Kubrick*. Paris, Calmann-Lévy.

Ciment, Michel (2003). *Kubrick: The Definitive Edition*. Faber & Faber.

Clarke, Artur C. (1968) *2001*, based on the screenplay by S. Kubrick & A.C. Clarke. London, Hutchinson.

Clarke, Artur C. (1951) *The Sentinel*. Avon Periodicals.

Cocks, Geoffrey (2004). *The wolf at the door: Stanley Kubrick, history, & the Holocaust*. P. Lang.

Cocks, Geoffrey; Diedrick, James; Perusek, Glenn (2006). *Depth of Field: Stanley Kubrick, Film, and the Uses of History*. Univ of Wisconsin Press.

Cohen, Alexander J. (1995) *Clockwork Orange and the Aestheticization of Violence.* Garnet Berkeley.

Coyle, Wallace (1980). *Stanley Kubrick, a guide to references and resources.* G. K. Hall.

Crone, Rainer (2013). *Stanley Kubrick: Drama & Shadows: Photographs 1945-1950*. Phaidon Press.

D'Alessandro, Emilio; Ulivieri, Filippo (2012). *Stanley Kubrick e me. Trent'anni accanto a lui. Rivelazioni e cronache inedite dell'assistente personale di un genio*. Il Saggiatore.

Deleuze, Gilles (1983). *L'image-mouvement*. Paris, Edition de Minuit.

Deleuze, Gilles (1985). *L'image-temps*. Paris, Edition de Minuit.

Delhomme, Jeanne (1969). *Nietzsche ou le voyageur et son ombre*. Paris, Seghers.

Domecq, Jean Philippe. Un voyage dans l'espace de Kubrick. *Positif*, February 1981, n° 239, p45-46

Duncan, Paul (2003). *Stanley Kubrick: Visual Poet 1928-1999*. Taschen.

Dupuy, Jean Paul (1987). En mal du père. *Positif*, October 1987, n° 320, p59-62.

Eisenschitz, Bernard (1969). La marge, 2001. *Cahiers du cinéma*, n° 209, February 1969, p56-57.

Falsetto, Mario (2001). *Stanley Kubrick: A Narrative and Stylistic Analysis*. Greenwood Publishing Group.

Falsetto, Mario (1996). *Perspectives on Stanley Kubrick*. G.K. Hall.

Felden, Thorsten (2007). *Man/Machine Interaction in the Work of Stanley Kubrick*. Grin Verlag.

Fischer, Ralf Michael (2009). *Raum und Zeit im filmischen*

Oeuvre von Stanley Kubrick. Berlin: Gebr. Mann Verlag.

Garsault, Alain (1981). Shining sous deux angles, 2) les deux visages du fantastique. *Positif*, January 1981, n° 238, p17-19

Gengaro, Christine Lee (2012). *Listening to Stanley Kubrick: The Music in His Films*. Rowman & Littlefield.

Gilliat, Penelope (1968). After Man. *The New Yorker*. April 13, 1968, p150

Giuliani, Pierre (1990). *Stanley Kubrick*. Francis Bordat, Paris, Rivages.

Granier, Jean (1982). *Nietzsche*. Paris, Presses Universitaires de France.

Greenberg, Harvey (1975). *The Movies on your mind*. p257-62

Harlan, Jan; Struthers, Jane M. (2009). *A. I. Artificial Intelligence: From Stanley Kubrick to Steven Spielberg - The Vision Behind the Film*. Thames & Hudson, Limited.

Hautecoeur, Louis (1954). *Symbolisme du cercle et de la coupole*. Picard & co,

Heide, Thomas von der (2006). *A Clockwork Orange - The presentation and the impact of violence in the novel and in the film*. GRIN Verlag.

Henry, Michael (1987). "Paint it Black", à propos de Full Metal Jacket. *Positif*, October 1987, n°320, p40-42

Homer. *L'Odyssée, poésie Homérique*. text translated by Victor Bérard, les belles lettres, 1924

Homer. *The Odyssey*. translated by T.E. Lawrence, Hertfordshire, Wordsworth Editions, 1992, 327p

Hughes, David (2013). *The Complete Kubrick*. Ebury Publishing.

Hunter, Tim. *2001, A Space Odyssey*. (with Stephen Kaplan & Peter Jasziis) The Harvard Crimson, 1968.

Jacke, Andreas (2009). *Stanley Kubrick: eine Deutung der Konzepte seiner Filme*. Psychosozial-Verlag.

Jameson, Fredric. *Signatures of the Visible*. Routledge, Chapman & Hall, 1990, p82-98.

Jenkins, Greg (1997). *Stanley Kubrick and the Art of Adaptation: Three Novels, Three Films*. McFarland.

Jost, François. *L'oeil-caméra, entre film et roman*. Lyon, Presses Universitaires de Lyon, 2nd edition 1989.

Kagan, Norman (2000). *Cinema of Stanley Kubrick: Third Edition*. Bloomsbury.

Kauffmann, Stanley (1968). Lost in the Stars. A review of "2001: A Space Odyssey." *The New Republic*, May 4, 1968

Kinney, Judy Lee (1982). *Text and pretext: Stanley Kubrick's adaptations*. University of California, Los Angeles.

Kolker, Robert (2006). *Stanley Kubrick's 2001: A Space Odyssey:New Essays*. Oxford University Press.

Koyré, Alexandre (1957). *Du monde clos à l'univers infini*,(translated from English by Raissa Tarr). Editions Gallimard, 1972 edition.

Krohn, Bill (1987). Le film-cerveau, Full Metal Jacket. *Cahiers du cinéma*, Oct 1987,n°400, p9-11

Kubrick, Stanley (1970). *A Clockwork Orange*. London, Hollywood Scripts.

Kubrick, Christiane (2002). *Stanley Kubrick: A Life in Pictures*. Bulfinch Press Book, Little, Brown.

LoBrutto, Vincent (1999). *Stanley Kubrick: A Biography*. Da Capo Press.

Lotman, Iouri (1973). *Sémiotique et esthétique du cinéma* (trad du russe par Sabine Breuillard). Ouvertures.

Löwith, Karl (1991). Nietzsche et la philosophie de l'éternel retour. Paris, Calmann-Lévy.

Mainar, Luis M. García (2000). *Narrative and Stylistice Patterns in the Films of Stanley Kubrick*. Camden House.

Masson, Alain (1981). Shining sous deux angles, 1) l'indifférence et le goût. *Positif*, January 1981, n° 238, p15-17

Mather, Philippe (2013). *Stanley Kubrick at Look Magazine: Authorship and Genre in Photojournalism and Film*. Intellect Ltd.

McDougal, Stuart Y. (2003). *Stanley Kubrick's A Clockwork Orange*. Cambridge University Press.

McQuiston, Kate (2013). *We'll Meet Again: Musical Design in the Films of Stanley Kubrick*. Oxford University Press.

Milon, Colette. Kubrick-Douglas, je t'aime moi non plus, les sentiers de la gloire. *VDN Magasine*, 1994

Modine, Matthew (2005). *Full Metal Jacket Diary*. Rugged Land.

Molina-Foix, Vicente (1981). Entretien avec Stanley

Kubrick. *Cahiers du cinéma*, January 1981, n° 319 p5-13

Monaco, James (1977). *How to read a film*. New York, Oxford University Press.

Nabokov, Vladimir (1955). *Lolita*. translated from English by E.H. Kahane, Paris, Gallimard, 1993 edition.

Nelson, Thomas Allen (1982). *Kubrick: Inside a Film's Artist's Maze*. Bloomington, Indiana University Press.

Nicholls, Peter (1984). *Fantastic cinema*. London, Ebury press,

Nietzsche, Friedrich (1883). *Thus Spoke Zathustra*. French edition, *Ainsi parlait Zarathoustra*. translated from German by Georges-Arthur Goldschmidt, Paris, Librairie Générale Française, 1983.

Oudart, Jean-Pierre (1978). A propos d'Orange Mécanique. Kubrick, Kramer et quelques autres, *Cahiers du cinéma*, n°293, Octobre 1978, p55-61

Oudart, Jean-Pierre (1976). Barry Lyndon. *Cahiers du Cinéma*, 1976, n° 271, p62

Oudart, Jean-Pierre (1980). Les inconnus dans la maison. *Cahiers du Cinéma*, Nov 1980, n° 317

Phillips, Gene D. (2001). *Stanley Kubrick: Interviews*. Univ. Press of Mississippi.

Pilard, Philippe (1990). *Barry Lyndon*. Paris, Synopsis Nathan.

Poulet, Georges (1961). *Les métamorphoses du cercle*. Paris, Plon.

Propp, Vladimir (1970). *Morphologie du conte* (trad. du russe par M. Derrida, T. Todorov, C. Cahn), Paris, Le Seuil.

Puiseux, Hélène (1988). *L'apocalypse nucléaire et son cinéma.* Paris, Les Editions du Cerf.

Rasmussen, Randy (2005). *Stanley Kubrick: Seven Films Analyzed.* McFarland.

Rhodes, Gary Don (2008). *Stanley Kubrick: essays on his films and legacy.* McFarland & Co.

Ruwe, Carolin (2007). *Symbols in Stanley Kubrick's Movie 'Eyes Wide Shut'.* GRIN Verlag.

Schill, Oliver (2004). *The expressionistic style and the theatricality in Stanley Kubrick's A Clockwork Orange (1971).* GRIN Verlag.

Schnitzler, Arthur (1926). *Traumnovelle* (Dream Story), Berlin, S. Fischer Verlag.

Schulze, Kerstin (2011). *A novel and its adaptation: Stanley Kubrick: Lolita (1962).* GRIN Verlag.

Sellier, Philippe (1970*). Le mythe du héros ou le désir d'être Dieu.* Paris-Montréal, Bordas.

Sineux, Michel (1981). Bye, Bye, Birdie-num-num (on Peter Sellers). *Positif*, February 1981, n° 239, p47-51

Sineux, Michel (1981). La symphonie Kubrick. *Positif*, February 1981, n° 239, p34-36

Stanford, W.B (1963). *The Ulysses Theme.* Oxford, Basil Blackwell, 2nd edition.

Tarnowski, Jean-François (1978). Approche et définition(s) du fantastique et de la science-fiction cinématographiques [II], *Positif*, 208-9, July 1978, p54-69

Thackeray, William Makepeace (1844). *Mémoires de Barry Lyndon du royaume d'Irlande*, translated from English by Léon de Wailly, Paris, Flammarion, 1990 edition.

Tobin, Yann (1987). Autopsie d'un genre, sur l'Ultime Razzia, *Positif*, October 1987, n° 320, p63-64

Vachaud, Laurent (1987). En attendant Kubrick, *Positif*, November 1987, n° 314 p2-9

Virilio, Paul (1987). Permis de détruire, Full Metal Jacket, *Cahiers du cinéma*, October 1987, n°400, p29-31

Volkmann, Maren (2006). *"A Clockwork Orange" in the Context of Subculture*. GRIN Verlag.

Walker, Alexander (1999). *Stanley Kubrick, Director. A Visual Analysis*. Harcourt Brace Co; Expanded edition

Webster, Patrick (2010). *Love and Death in Kubrick: A Critical Study of the Films from Lolita through Eyes Wide Shut*. McFarland.

Wheat, Leonard F. (2000). *Kubrick's 2001: A Triple Allegory*. Scarecrow Press.

Index

2001: A Space Odyssey, 9, 14, 16, 21, 22, 26, 28, 30, 31, 33, 34, 37, 38, 42, 44, 61, 62, 64, 68, 74, 75, 79, 81, 82, 83, 84, 85, 87, 89, 90, 96, 98, 99, 103, 104, 106, 109, 110, 113, 120, 124, 125

A woman under the influence, 69

abstraction, 30, 102, 118

action, 73, 89, 101, 112, 113

adventures, 12, 13, 67, 89, 112, 115

aesthetic, 20, 122
  aesthetical, 21
  aestheticization, 43, 51

Agnosticism, 31

alchemy, 31, 118

Alex, 21, 22, 23, 38, 39, 41, 42, 48, 52, 54, 56, 58, 62, 72, 75, 76, 77, 78, 81, 84, 87, 88, 89, 96, 97, 99, 104, 111, 122, 125, 127

Ambassador de Sadesky, 85, 88

American, 5, 27, 70, 73, 83, 120, 124, 157

amphibology, 83

analytical, 66

Angelopoulos Théo, 14

angles, 76, 91

animal, 23, 25, 72, 98, 113
  animosity, 87

Ant Hill, 48, 49

antagonist, 84, 99

anthropoids, 26

anti-Americanism, 71

anti-hero, 87
  antiheroes, 71

anti-militarism, 71

antithesis, 79

Antoninus, 22, 95

Antonioni Michelangelo, 73

anxiety, 70

apes, 87

Apocalypse now, 70

Arbogast, 69
arena, 46
army, 72
   Army, 85
art, 37, 53, 63, 118, 119, 121
astronauts, 28, 34, 86, 87, 106
attraction, 58
audience, 47, 62, 66, 70, 73, 82, 111, 113, 116, 118, 122
avant-garde, 73, 91
Barry Lyndon, 16, 21, 22, 28, 40, 44, 48, 52, 54, 55, 57, 63, 71, 75, 79, 81, 83, 89, 90, 96, 97, 103, 104, 119, 122
bathrooms, 77
Batianus, 77
battleground, 53
Beauty, 52
Bernardi Sandro, 17, 54, 65, 73, 82, 96, 107, 109, 110, 112, 113, 114, 115, 116, 117, 119, 121, 124, 130
birth, 23, 38, 41, 43, 118
body, 28, 38, 74, 83, 84, 111, 124
bone, 25, 26, 27, 76, 85
books, 4
Bowman, 18, 21, 22, 25, 29, 30, 32, 33, 34, 38, 39, 40, 48, 67, 76, 77, 78, 81, 85, 87, 90, 99, 104, 110, 118, 125
boxing, 77
brain, 30, 42, 45, 67, 85, 86
breathing, 87
Brian, 22, 89
Brooklyn, 3, 4
Broulard, 48, 54, 78
brutality, 76, 104
Buñuel Luis, 73
Burgess Anthony, 84
Byron, 12
Byronic, 13
Cahiers du cinéma, 107, 111, 112, 116, 125, 126, 131, 132, 135, 136, 138
Calderón, 12
Calypso, 43
camera, 43, 48, 49, 53, 54, 55, 56, 72, 80, 91, 111, 122
Camp Climax, 88
Captain Potzdorf, 78
Captain Quin, 57
Cartier Walter, 82
Cassavetes John, 69
Cat Lady, 48, 58, 89
catastrophism, 71

cathartis, 80, 92, 121
Catholic Legion of
   Decency, 88
cave, 25, 28, 43, 62, 66,
   76, 79, 92, 97, 111
caves, 45, 61, 66, 98
celestial, 25, 37, 44, 80,
   125
celestial sphere, 25
cell, 83, 84, 85, 86, 107
Cellularity, 86
censored, 127
censure, 72
centrifugal, 12, 41, 105
centripetal, 12, 14, 41
cerebral, 65, 113
Chaplin, 118
Chaplin Charlie, 15
Chapman, 12
character, 56, 76
characters, 20, 22, 40,
   45, 46, 49, 53, 57, 58,
   82, 83, 84, 125
Charlotte Haze, 48
chateau, 47, 53
chess, 15, 47, 48, 108
Chess, 47
chessboard, 15, 47, 77,
   96
childhood, 44, 85, 87,
   124
Christ, 38, 73
Christian, 38
chronologically, 75

church, 81, 84
Ciment Michel, 14, 25,
   30, 34, 44, 50, 72, 83,
   96, 98, 99, 102, 103,
   105, 107, 109, 117,
   118, 120, 121, 123,
   124, 125, 131
Cimino Michael, 71
cinema, 59, 62, 63, 72,
   73, 87, 90, 92, 110,
   114, 115, 116, 118,
   121, 124
Cinema, 13, 114
cinematic, 17, 47, 48,
   53, 61, 111, 117, 118
cinematographic, 9, 14,
   15, 17, 61, 65, 67, 74,
   91, 101, 112, 118
cinematography, 18
Circe, 57
circle, 14, 20, 39, 42, 43,
   44, 45, 46, 48, 49, 52,
   55, 96, 107, 120, 124
Circle, 51, 124
circles, 43, 44, 45, 52,
   107, 108, 120
circular, 14, 17, 20, 22,
   23, 27, 34, 39, 40, 43,
   44, 45, 46, 48, 49, 51,
   58, 80, 91, 103, 108,
   120, 124
circularity, 14, 16, 20,
   22, 43, 48, 116, 120
Circularity, 48

circumference, 20, 39, 44, 47, 51, 100
civilization, 87
Clarke Arthur C., 18, 31 44, 102, 110, 113
classic, 73, 115
    classical, 67, 69, 73, 91
Clean Break, 68
clichés, 70
Clockwork Orange, 16, 21, 22, 43, 48, 52, 54, 56, 58, 62, 63, 72, 75, 78, 79, 81, 83, 84, 88, 93, 96, 97, 99, 117, 120, 127, 130, 131, 133, 135, 137, 138
codes, 84, 87, 115
    codification, 85, 86
coincidence, 56, 102
Colonel Dax, 21, 77
color, 83, 90, 111
columns, 46
communicate, 84, 86
communication, 84, 87, 123
communications, 85
computer, 81, 124, 125
concave, 56
connotative, 87
conscience, 30, 50, 74, 112
consciousness, 31, 37, 39, 45, 61, 62
constellation, 64, 116
contemporary, 73, 91, 102
convex, 56
Cook Elisha, 68
Coppola Francis Ford, 70
corpse, 84
Cosmatos George, 71
cosmic, 65, 87, 113
Crassus, 57, 78
creation, 64, 69, 73
criticism, 69, 71, 73, 119
Cruise Tom, 22
curve, 49, 53, 56
cyclical, 20, 39, 106
Cyclop, 25, 67
Cyclopean, 64
Cyclops, 67
Daedalus, 50
Dalila, 57
Danny, 22, 42, 44, 49, 50, 51, 69, 76, 82, 106, 107
Danny Torrance, 22
Dante, 12
Darwin, 25
Dave Bowman, 21
David Bowman, 25
Davy, 21, 40, 48, 57, 76, 80, 89, 97, 110, 122

Davy Gordon, 21, 40
Dawn of Man, 104
Dax, 47, 48
Day of the Fight, 82
de Laurentiis Dino, 14
De Mille Cecil B, 73
death, 16, 27, 33, 34, 38, 39, 53, 80, 89, 104, 107, 112, 123, 126
deconstructionist, 70
deconstructive, 17, 70
de-humanizing, 24
Deleuze Gilles, 17, 30, 65, 96, 99, 113, 132
demiurgic eye, 21
Demme Jonathan, 74
depredation, 56
desire, 14, 37, 89
destiny, 20, 30, 32, 58, 101, 117, 121
destruction, 27, 34, 67, 83
dialogues, 89, 90, 101, 126
dimensionality, 45
dimensions, 70
Direct references, 75
director, 21, 43, 51, 52, 63, 65, 89, 91
discourse, 73, 116
Discovery, 25, 30, 44, 107
discussion, 85, 107
dissolution, 83, 124

distorted, 82, 83, 92
distortion, 83
divine, 29, 32, 37, 65
Divinities, 20
dolly movement, 54
dolly movements, 91, 102
Doomsday, 27, 49, 106
double, 40, 47, 73, 80, 81, 82, 87, 97, 100, 101, 108, 122, 123
double-entendres, 87
Douglas Kirk, 95
Dr Strangelove, 82, 108, 120
Dr. Strangelove, 16, 21, 27, 49, 71, 75, 80, 82, 84, 85, 87, 89, 98, 106, 108, 126
Draba, 48
Dracula, 72, 109
dramatic, 67, 101
dream, 29, 46, 57, 58, 112, 122
droog, 75, 76, 84
Droog, 23
dualism, 71, 79
duel, 22, 57, 125
duels, 77, 96
Dun Laoghaire, 48
dystopian, 84
earth, 28, 33, 75, 82, 102, 103, 124

Earth, 32, 79, 95, 98, 113
Easter Island, 64
effect, 53, 69, 81, 92, 113, 114
Eisenstein, 118
Eisenstein Sergei, 15
ellipsis, 26, 38, 69
ellipsoidal logic, 20
empathy, 53
Enchanted Hunters Hotel, 88
enemy, 71, 72
English, 84
epic, 11, 20, 30, 37, 38
epic cycle, 20
epitome, 25, 30
eternal, 29, 37, 38, 39, 41
Eternal Return, 39, 40, 41, 42, 58
eternity, 39, 41, 43, 112
Eternity, 43
Europe, 79
Eve, 57
evolutionary, 25, 26, 27
execution, 86
experimental, 73
experimentation, 17, 91
exploration, 30, 107
extraterrestrial, 31, 64
eye, 17, 48, 50, 52, 53, 83, 111, 116, 119

eyes, 38, 57, 76, 105, 114, 117
Eyes Wide Shut, 16, 39, 46, 57, 58, 63, 71, 89, 93, 126, 127, 129, 137, 138
fantasies, 89
fate, 23, 39, 48, 58
fear, 33, 70, 96, 113
Fear and Desire, 16, 32, 71, 82, 83, 100
feminine, 123
feminist, 57
fetus, 34, 101, 124
filiation, 29
film, 4, 9, 14, 15, 16, 17, 26, 30, 39, 43, 44, 45, 58, 61, 62, 66, 68, 70, 72, 74, 75, 78, 82, 89, 92, 95, 97, 100, 104, 107, 108, 109, 113, 114, 115, 117, 120, 121, 123, 125, 126
film noir, 68
fixity, 83
Floyd, 38, 85, 104
force, 12, 86, 105, 123
form, 4, 13, 18, 40, 49, 51, 82, 83, 90, 98, 115, 117, 118, 119
forms, 17, 53, 66, 73, 79, 83, 115, 116, 118, 122, 124, 125

Fragmentation, 84
France, 9, 158
freedom, 16, 21, 23, 42, 56, 57, 71, 106
French, 57, 81, 108
Freud Sigmund, 70, 116
  Freudian, 30
Fuchs Ernst, 64
Full Metal Jacket, 16, 21, 24, 49, 58, 70, 71, 76, 78, 79, 83, 86, 88, 106, 117, 120, 125, 126
future, 42, 79, 121, 124
gangster literature, 68
gargantuan, 88
General Buck Turgidson, 81, 88
General Turgidson, 86
genre, 11, 67, 68, 69, 70
geometric, 86
  geometrical, 34
  geometry, 53
George, 39, 57, 126
German, 57
ghost, 87, 97, 105
ghosts, 46, 102
Giraudoux Jean 12
gladiators, 47, 99
Gloria, 57, 76, 80, 122
God, 31, 32, 37, 64, 100, 112, 125
Godard Jean-Luc, 74
gods, 28, 29, 103

Goethe, 12
Gothic, 70
Gracchus, 57, 78
Grady, 46, 106, 108
Greece, 13
  Greek, 23, 30
  Greeks, 20
Griffith D. W., 15
Gulliver's Travels, 86
Hades, 24, 108
HAL, 30, 37, 38, 48, 50, 67, 77, 82, 85, 87, 98, 106, 125
  Hal 9000, 25
hallucinations, 69
Hamlet, 44, 90
Handycam, 55
Harford Bill, 28, 38, 41, 46, 71
Hartman, 24, 78, 84, 86, 87
Hawks Howard, 68
Hayden Sterling, 68
Heaven, 31
hegemonic, 27, 32
  hegemony, 34
helicoid movement, 51
Heracles, 38
hero, 12, 20, 37, 38, 39, 40, 55, 58, 71, 87, 95, 96, 97, 104
  heroes, 17, 40
  heroism, 37
  hero's journey, 20

Heywood Floyd, 26
Hilton space station, 27
Hogarth William, 52, 53, 54, 109
Hollywood, 15, 71, 72, 101, 110, 119
Homer, 11, 13, 14, 22, 28, 29, 95, 99
   Homeric, 11, 30, 95, 99
homo sapiens, 27
humanoids, 26
Humbert, 21, 38, 41, 47, 48, 49, 50, 55, 56, 57, 75, 77, 81, 89, 101, 109, 110, 120, 123, 126
   Humbert Humbert, 21, 50, 57, 81
Huston John, 68
iconographic, 63
identity, 33, 86
imagination, 43, 70, 95, 100, 121
immobility, 54
   ... immobilization, 63
immortality, 42, 84
indirect references, 75
infinity, 31, 32, 61, 112
information, 4, 15, 72
innovations, 68, 90
intelligence, 64, 118
intensity, 91

intergalactic, 29, 61
interpretation, 20, 26, 31, 64, 113
introspective, 82
Ireland, 22, 40, 97
irony, 71
island, 14, 33, 86
Italy, 13
Ithaca, 14, 91, 92
Jack, 21, 22, 39, 40, 41, 42, 43, 45, 46, 50, 55, 56, 58, 63, 66, 69, 70, 75, 76, 81, 85, 87, 88, 102, 104, 106, 107, 108, 122
Jack D. Ripper, 21, 50, 85, 88
jail, 46, 47, 63, 108
jargon, 27, 84, 85
Jazz, 15
jealousy, 80
Johnny Clay, 21, 89, 122
Johnson Diane, 70
Joker, 21, 41, 56, 76, 78, 89
journey, 12, 14, 21, 29, 30, 31, 50, 51, 62, 80, 122, 123, 125
Joyce James 12, 14, 37, 95
judges, 47, 108
Jupiter, 62, 80, 104

Jupiter Mission, 104
juxtaposition, 20, 43, 54
Kafka Franz, 69
  Kafkaian, 49
Kane Charles Foster, 69
Kazantzakis Nikos 12
Khatchaturian Aram 34
Kidman Nicole, 89
Killer's Kiss, 16, 21, 23, 40, 48, 57, 80, 83, 89
King Stephen, 69, 70
knowledge, 16, 29, 33, 34, 47, 64, 119
Korova Milkbar, 76
Koyré Alexandre, 34, 103, 110
Kubrick Stanley, 4, 9, 14, 15, 16, 17, 18, 20, 21, 23, 26, 28, 29, 30, 31, 32, 33, 34, 37, 38, 40, 41, 43, 47, 48, 49, 51, 52, 53, 56, 58, 61, 62, 63, 65, 66, 67, 68, 69, 70, 71, 72, 73, 74, 77, 78, 79, 80, 81, 82, 83, 84, 87, 89, 90, 91, 92, 95, 96, 97, 98, 99, 100, 101, 102, 105, 106, 107, 108, 109, 110, 111, 112, 113, 114, 115, 116, 117, 118, 119, 120, 121, 122, 123, 124, 125, 126
Kubrickian, 20, 22, 37, 38, 39, 43, 49, 50, 51, 55, 61, 62, 64, 69, 72, 74, 78, 80, 82, 87, 89, 91, 92, 120
La niña, 73
laboratory, 31
labyrinth, 49, 50, 55, 70, 92
Lady Lyndon, 38, 57, 78, 81, 90
language, 14, 17, 53, 84, 86, 87, 89, 90, 91, 95, 101, 102, 112, 122
  language regression, 87
Laputa, 86, 88
Le regard d'Ulysse, 14
Lieutenant Lockart, 72
Ligeti György, 67, 135
light, 24, 33, 81, 83, 92, 108, 110, 113, 116, 118, 122
line, 13, 28, 43, 48, 51, 52, 53, 56, 57, 58, 79, 87, 108, 112
linguistic, 84, 85, 125
literature, 67, 68, 69, 70
Lolita, 16, 21, 22, 38, 47, 48, 52, 57, 73, 75, 81, 82, 83, 87, 88, 101, 109, 123, 125, 126
London, 15, 79, 117

love, 15, 32, 57, 58, 63, 89, 96, 99
  love scene, 63
Lovecraft H. P., 70
Ludovico, 24, 41, 58, 62, 75
  Ludovico technique, 58, 62, 75
lunar, 25, 27, 104
machines, 24, 37, 98, 106
madness, 56, 70, 77, 82, 104, 107, 119
Magritte, 65
Major T.J. "King" Kong, 88
man, 13, 16, 18, 25, 26, 27, 30, 31, 32, 33, 34, 37, 42, 58, 76, 79, 92, 98, 101, 102, 106, 113
  Man, 25, 26, 27, 33, 81, 98, 101, 104, 115, 119
Manichaeism, 71
manipulation, 62, 87
map, 65, 66
  map of Tendre, 66
Marcellus, 78
Marines, 24, 58, 84, 89
masculine, 45, 57, 58, 123
mask, 64
  masks, 46

mathematical, 64
maze, 30, 40, 43, 49, 50, 51, 54, 55, 63, 66, 79, 107, 108, 109
meaning, 17, 21, 26, 28, 55, 62, 64, 66, 70, 73, 83, 90, 114, 122
Mecca, 64
mechanism, 41, 44, 56, 58, 71, 79, 85, 106, 118
memory, 40, 67
Messiah, 31
metamorphosis, 28, 44, 92, 118
Mickey Club, 24
microcosmic, 74
military, 21, 24, 47, 81, 85, 86, 106
millenary, 26, 61, 104
Mireau, 47, 48, 53, 77, 78
mirror, 51, 65, 80, 81, 82, 102, 114, 122, 123
  mirroring effect, 81
modern, 13, 15, 34, 73, 79, 91, 119
  modernity, 79
monolith, 18, 26, 27, 32, 38, 61, 63, 64, 65, 71, 80, 81, 85, 110, 112, 113, 114
monologues, 87

moon, 44, 75
Moonwatcher, 26, 27, 61, 62, 76, 80
moral codes, 73
mortality, 37
Mosaic, 64
motion, 16, 17, 20, 22, 51, 52, 53, 55

movement, 16, 17, 20, 21, 23, 28, 38, 39, 42, 43, 48, 49, 51, 52, 53, 54, 56, 92, 107, 118
movie, 34, 38, 61, 65, 69, 72, 78, 81, 124
  movie theatres, 61
  movies, 15, 20, 38, 48, 67, 68, 69, 73, 83, 89, 113, 124
  motion pictures, 17, 20
Mr. Swine, 88
Murnau F. W., 15, 69
music, 9, 24, 34, 106
  musical, 15, 67, 80, 86, 91, 102
myth, 37, 39, 71, 101, 118, 121
  mythical, 17, 21, 34, 38, 43, 70
  myths, 30, 37, 39, 121
Nabokov, 47
Nadsat, 84, 125

narration, 17, 21, 40, 67, 73, 113, 116
narrative, 12, 13, 30, 43, 66, 67, 70, 73, 89, 95, 101, 115, 116
  narrative cinema, 74
narrator, 15, 24, 40, 89
Nature, 20, 52, 56
Navajo, 44, 107
  Navajo circle, 45, 107
negation, 89, 90
negatives, 83
Nelson T.A., 66, 74, 82, 98, 107, 108, 109, 115, 119, 122, 123
New York, 3, 4, 5, 9, 15, 111, 158
Nietzsche, 12, 25, 28, 30, 39, 40, 98, 99, 100, 103, 105
  Nietzschean, 25, 26, 101
Nora, 57
objectivity, 30
observatory, 31
occult, 63, 69, 89
Odyssean, 11, 13, 14, 16, 18, 20, 21, 22, 43, 46, 51, 73, 91, 116, 120
  Odyssean theme, 13, 14, 43, 51, 91
  Odysseanity, 17

Odysseus, 13, 14, 20, 22, 23, 24, 25, 29, 34, 39, 40, 41, 43, 51, 57, 58, 79, 91, 99, 105, 115
Odyssey, 11, 13, 14, 15, 16, 17, 20, 23, 28, 29, 30, 32, 34, 38, 40, 41, 44, 49, 50, 55, 57, 58, 61, 62, 65, 66, 67, 74, 90, 92, 97, 99, 106
oedipal, 44
oedipal triangle, 44
Olympia, 14
Olympian, 47
omnipresent, 38, 72, 84
Ophüls Max, 15, 118
oppressed, 78, 79
oppressor, 78
Orion, 44
ornament, 20, 40
Overlook Hotel, 41, 45, 49, 55, 69, 70, 105
painting, 45, 75, 83, 91, 119
parable, 28, 31, 96
parallaxes, 91
paranoia, 47, 100
parody, 87, 109
Parris Island, 24, 86, 120, 125
Pascal Blaise, 32, 33, 101
passion, 66, 107, 118

past, 40, 42, 55, 79, 107, 118, 121, 124
paths, 52, 66
Paths of Glory, 16, 21, 22, 47, 49, 52, 53, 57, 71, 78, 83
Paul Valéry, 40
Penelope, 14, 57, 58, 99
peregrination, 13, 51, 57, 86
perpendicular, 53
phallus, 88, 127
philosophical, 21, 62, 82
photogrammic, 40, 63
photograph, 40, 45, 72
photography, 15, 91
pictorialism, 15, 83
pictures, 62, 67, 71, 72, 73, 83, 112, 119, 120
Plato, 62
Platonician, 62
Pleistocene, 26, 61, 104
pluricephal, 91
poem, 81, 100, 102
poetry, 88
police, 84
politicians, 23, 84, 97
poltergeists, 45, 108
Poole, 22, 25, 28, 48, 81, 85
Poseidon, 23, 58
Positif, 96, 97, 102, 103, 106, 117, 120, 129,

130, 131, 132, 133, 135, 137, 138
premier Kissoff, 88
Primal Man, 13
prisoner, 58, 111
prisons, 46
private Pyle, 39
process, 27, 40, 42, 46, 69, 75, 79, 106
production, 15, 73
Production Code, 88
progression, 31
Promethean, 37, 103
propaganda, 71, 73
Prussia, 22
Psyche, 51
Psycho, 69
psychological, 62, 70, 82, 87, 122
Pyle, 76, 78, 86, 126
questioning, 17, 39, 63, 73, 91
Quilty, Clare, 18, 22, 47, 48, 75, 77, 81, 87, 110, 120, 123, 126
Rabelaisian, 88
rage, 76, 100
Rambo, 71
Rapallo, 57, 76, 80, 97
reality, 37, 53, 72, 83, 89, 111, 117
rebirth, 23, 24, 37, 38, 104, 107
Redmond, 48, 57
reference, 33, 67, 69, 99, 127
references, 75, 76, 98
referential, 18, 34, 63, 67, 68, 72, 74, 75, 78
reflection, 80, 81, 117, 122, 125
reflective, 63, 64, 82
regressions, 87
relationships, 86
replication, 80
representation, 14, 37, 44, 51, 73, 86, 116
return, 12, 14, 16, 20, 21, 22, 23, 39, 40, 41, 42, 46, 49, 50, 51, 52, 58, 71, 83, 87, 90, 92, 96, 97, 98, 101, 105, 109, 116
  Return movement, 21
  Return of Odysseus, 14, 41, 58
revelation, 30, 89, 91
reverse shots, 91
Robinson, 42
robotic, 85
Roget, 47, 53
Roman, 46, 48, 76
room, 15, 30, 32, 33, 34, 47, 49, 63, 72, 79, 81, 85, 100, 103, 110, 118, 121
rotation, 41
Russians, 27, 85, 88

satirical, 71
scenario, 20, 68
schizophrenia, 79, 82
Science-Fiction, 68
scientists, 27, 84, 85
Scorsese Martin, 74
screen, 39, 47, 61, 64, 69, 74, 81, 110, 111, 122, 124
self-delusion, 56
Sellers Peter, 82
semantic, 63
senator, 76
serpentine, 52, 53, 109
Serpentine, 56
sex, 79, 88, 126
Sex, 127
sexual, 41, 44, 48, 57, 58, 71, 87, 88, 89, 123, 126
sexuality, 87
Shakespeare, 12
shape, 57, 95
Sherry, 57
ship, 29, 87
shots, 15, 49, 55, 63, 81, 91
silence, 85, 91, 114
silent, 33, 85, 87, 89, 90
silent film, 90
sinuosity, 14, 56
   sinuous, 14, 15, 51, 52, 53, 55, 56, 58, 110
   sinuous line, 14, 51, 52, 55, 56
slaves, 22, 46, 82, 120
Slavic, 84
solar, 38, 39, 120
soldiers, 47, 53, 57, 86, 100
sounds, 90, 116, 121
soundtrack, 62
space, 4, 9, 14, 16, 18, 20, 25, 27, 29, 32, 33, 40, 44, 45, 46, 48, 54, 62, 63, 76, 79, 80, 82, 85, 87, 91, 99, 105, 106, 107, 108, 112, 122
   spatial, 34, 41, 50, 55, 91, 106
   spatiotemporal, 26, 32 spatio-temporality, 17
space station, 40
   space-pod, 76
   spaceship, 25, 26, 30, 38, 44, 107
Spartacus, 16, 21, 22, 23, 41, 46, 48, 57, 73, 75, 76, 77, 78, 82, 83, 89, 95, 99, 120
spectator, 18, 58, 62, 67, 68, 69, 71, 72, 73, 74, 77, 78, 80, 89, 92, 114, 119

speech, 85, 87, 114
sphere, 31, 37, 38, 40, 44, 100
  spherical, 20, 47
spiraling, 51, 91
spiritualistic, 87
Stanford W.B., 95
Star-Child, 25, 29, 31, 38, 40, 63, 75, 92
Stars and Stripes, 72
Steadycam, 55
stereotypes, 70
stone, 64, 113
Stonehenge, 64
story, 40, 83, 105, 112, 125
strangeness, 70, 116
strategic, 21, 80
Straus Johan, 28, 42
Strick Joseph, 14
structure, 11, 37, 39, 67, 68, 70, 74, 114, 125
stylization, 17, 43, 51
subconscious, 61, 110
subject, 67, 69, 71, 79, 84, 87, 111, 120
subjectivity, 30
Sun, 38, 104, 113
Superman, 25, 26, 28, 101
surrealist, 53
Swift Jonathan, 86
symbol, 44, 50, 56, 64, 112, 117

symbolization, 23, 63
symmetrical, 34, 55
symmetry, 26, 40, 56, 81, 97
tapestry, 91
Tarkovsky Andrei, 74
techniques, 91, 118
technology, 25
Telemachus, 22, 29
telepathic, 76, 87
television, 72
temporal, 32, 40, 41, 50, 53, 54, 96, 116
  temporality, 40
Têt, 86
The Asphalt Jungle, 68
The Big Sleep, 68
The Deer Hunter, 71
The Exorcist, 69
The Green Berets, 71
The Killing, 16, 21, 39, 57, 68, 83, 89
The Maltese Falcon, 68
The Shining, 16, 21, 22, 44, 46, 49, 50, 55, 63, 66, 69, 79, 81, 83, 86, 89, 102, 105, 109, 116, 117, 120
theatres, 15, 127
Theseus, 50
thesis, 30, 79
Thrace, 23
time, 18, 20, 21, 29, 30, 39, 40, 41, 42, 43, 45,

46, 48, 52, 53, 54, 66, 76, 80, 90, 91, 97, 101, 102, 105, 106, 109, 112, 118, 122, 123
times, 15, 39, 46, 83
tone, 85
tool, 27, 84
topography, 53
topos, 30
tracking, 53
transcendental, 31
transmissions, 85
trap, 64
traveler, 24, 66, 68, 74, 78
Tree of Knowledge, 64
trenches, 52, 53
Troy, 24
Übermensch, 25, 98
ultra-violence, 79, 84
Ulysses, 11, 12, 13, 14, 95
uncensored, 127
underworld, 45, 46, 57, 104
United States, 79, 127, 158
unity, 52, 79, 124
universe, 18, 27, 32, 33, 34, 46, 49, 61, 62, 74, 78, 79, 80, 83, 85, 91, 102, 115, 120, 121

vacuum, 62
variety, 37, 52, 53
verbal, 13, 69, 87
verticality, 46
victimizers, 77
Victims, 77
Victorian, 63
Viennese waltz, 42
Viet Cong, 58
Vietnam, 22, 24, 49, 67, 70, 72, 117, 126
Vietnam war, 49, 67, 70
violence, 73, 79, 81, 84
Virgil, 12
vision, 17, 53, 59, 90, 113, 114, 115, 116, 117
visionary, 15, 86
visual experience, 61, 115
Voice-over, 89
voyage, 30, 50, 51, 68, 102, 105, 108, 116
voyagers, 46
voyeur, 81
voyeurism, 80
war, 27, 41, 49, 68, 70, 71, 72, 85, 101, 103, 117, 121
war film, 70
war pictures, 71
Warner Bros, 127
war-room, 86

Wayne John, 71
weapon, 27, 76, 84, 85, 99, 125
Welles, 124
Welles Orson, 15
Wenders Wim, 73
Wendy, 58, 69, 72, 77, 108
wheel, 28, 29, 40, 41, 42, 44, 92
wheelchairs, 77
White Lionel, 68
wisdom, 64

woman, 53, 57, 68, 69, 72
women, 43, 46, 57, 58, 89
Words, 90
world, 16, 21, 24, 27, 29, 30, 34, 37, 41, 42, 45, 49, 61, 65, 75, 79, 80, 82, 83, 92, 97, 102, 103, 107, 108, 111, 119, 121
Zarathustra, 25, 28, 29, 30, 98, 103

About the Author

Fabrice Jaumont is the author of *Unequal Partners: American Foundations and Higher Education Development in Africa* (Palgrave-MacMillan, 2016); *The Bilingual Revolution: The Future of Education is in Two Languages* (TBR Books, 2017); and *Partenaires inégaux. Fondations américaines et universités en Afrique* (Editions de la Maison des sciences de l'homme, 2018)

A native of France, Fabrice Jaumont moved to the United States in 1997. He is currently a Program Director for FACE Foundation in New York, and Education Attaché for the Embassy of France to the United States. He is also a Senior Fellow at Fondation Maison des Sciences de l'Homme in Paris. Fabrice Jaumont holds a Ph.D. in Comparative and International Education from New York University.

In recognition of his various involvements in education and culture, Fabrice Jaumont was honored with several awards including the Cultural Diversity Award; the Academic Palms; and the Medal of Honor. His work received the accolades of various news media. For the author's blog, visit fabricejaumont.net

www.ingramcontent.com/pod-product-compliance
Lightning Source LLC
Chambersburg PA
CBHW030525080526
44586CB00011B/326